Y0-CSH-585
Cernuschi, Alberto/The constructive mani
HX542 .C43 1983 C.1 STACKS 1983

25340

HX
542      Cernuschi, Alberto
C43
1983     The constructive manifesto

**DATE DUE**

| JUN 25 2001 | | | |
|---|---|---|---|
| JUL 10 2003 | | | |
| | | | |
| | | | |
| | | | |
| | | | |
| | | | |
| | | | |
| | | | |
| | | | |
| | | | |
| | | | |

# THE CONSTRUCTIVE MANIFESTO

By The Same Author:

*THEORY OF AUTODEISM*
*LIFE AND VOYAGES OF CENTURY*
*EXISTENCE ON TRIAL*
*MACBETH STEEL*
*HARRY FRANK MADE IT!*
*BURN HIM ON THE STAKE! (GIORDANO BRUNO)*


In preparation:

*EAST COAST, WEST COAST AND ELSEWHERE*

# THE CONSTRUCTIVE MANIFESTO

by
Alberto Cernuschi

Philosophical Library
New York

Library of Congress Cataloging in Publication Data

Cernuschi, Alberto.
    The constructive manifesto.

   1. Communism and society. 2. Marx, Karl,
1818-1883. I. Title.
HX542.C43 1983   335.43   82-18903
ISBN 0-8022-2411-3


Copyright 1983 by Philosophical Library, Inc.
200 West 57th Street, New York, N.Y. 10019.
All rights reserved.

Manufactured in the United States of America.

# PREFACE

Envisioning a better world probably began soon after the development of language. Some visions involved a singular change — perhaps the development of agriculture, or a new tax structure, e.g. Henry George's single tax or the graduated income tax. Others have involved a complete restructuring of society, witness the numerous utopias and the visions of modern ideologists; nationalist, classical liberal, marxist, socialist and liberationist. Of course, there were also solutions proposed by ancient and modern religious leaders. Although many have had an impact, the quest for a way to provide universal freedom, justice and peace continues.

New technologies and demographics render some visions impossible, but at the same time create new possibilities. Jefferson's ideal of a nation of farmers and Gandhi's ideal of a nation of economically self-sufficient villages were, if not impossible when pronounced, at least rendered obsolete shortly thereafter. On the other hand, nation-states and world government were inconceivable until man could communicate and travel expeditiously.

Alberto Cernuschi's approach to a better world is a secular one. It involves domestic refocusing and international restructuring. It is partially pragmatic, yet he remarks that "a turnaround completely changing our values and goals is imperative." It is an integrative vision blending elements of humanism, liberalism, rationalism, and governmental universalism.

To some of the specific elements of this view I shall return shortly, but attention must first be given to the subject which comprises the earlier part of the book: Marx and Marxism. The author has almost written two seperate books. The first five chapters deal with the Communist Manifesto, Marx's associated writings, and Marx himself. The last two chapters deal with the need for and the nature of his Constructive Manifesto.

Roughly one-third of the world's population lives under leaders who legitimatize their rule by the Communist Manifesto. This stimulates Cernuschi to criticize Marx's ideas on analytical and pragmatic grounds. His theories have been debunked by many and often, yet Cernuschi's approach — although not comprehensive — is direct and fresh. He does not bother much with its Hegelian structure, for instance. Rather he stresses contradictions, historical inaccuracies, predictive deficiencies, and distortions in practice.

Although Marx frequently chastized the bourgeoisie, he shows implicit praise for them for their ability to subjugate nature and increase production. At the same time he shows that Marx's criticism of the bourgeoisie is even more applicable to the government of the Soviet Union: the policy of concentrating capital, the prevalence of subsistence wages, etc. He argues that Marx's assumption of a two-class structure was false then, and is even less true today.

Cernuschi contrasts the Marxist principles with practices in the Soviet Union. Marx expected to provide a new order which would make the masses happy. The author describes what was produced instead: underproduction, scarcity, low worker productivity in agriculture, heavy indebtedness to Western banks, managerial inefficiency, oppressiveness, nationalism instead of universal class consciousness, a controlled press, managerial class luxury, forced labor, show trials, and other abuses of the populace. He observes that the Soviet government seems unwilling or incapable of making necessary economic changes without outside assistance.

These conclusions are probably incontrovertible. I would welcome a discussion of practices in other communist systems (China, Cuba, East Europe, Vietnam, and North Korea), and also a discussion of some matters which the Soviets claim to be positive achievements: a lower level of unemployment than in the West, and a higher growth rate over the past couple of decades; the expansion of land cultivation; the emphasis on the production of military goods.

Particularly interesting is Cernuschi's description of Marx's personal development and personality: his hatred of religion and the middle class, the occasional disparagement of Jews although his father was a Jew until his conversion to Christianity, his drinking and deference to men and women with status and money, his difficulty in achieving any of his professional goals, his apparently sizeable ego and his treachery toward supporters if they no longer furthered his literary and political career. His relationship with Engels, Bakunin, and other communists of the period is discussed. Cernuschi does not center on an explanation of why Marx was what he was, but his vivid account does help to explain why he developed a blusterous writing style, a violent revolutionary philosophy, and why he had difficulty developing personal relationships of mutual trust.

After discussing the obsolescence of Marxist thought the author turns to the contemporary yearning for an orientation more befitting our time. Although he sympathizes with our young revolutionaries because of their idealism and vision, he thinks that they are too negative and lack a cohesive program. His purpose is to provide one: one that is non-dogmatic and predominantly humanistic.

*The Constructive Manifesto* places great confidence in ideas and the power of human will. It does not present detailed plans on how we might achieve a better world; rather the emphasis is on the necessary attitudes and guidelines. It is closer to the idealistic school of classical liberalism than the realistic one in that many social goals are left open to the society.

It urges us to improve without destroying, and to concentrate on a positive attitude rather than a negative one. It urges us to rehabilitate utopian visions and, to whatever extent possible, eliminate meaningless, obsolete phraseology which induces hate. Government should regulate and direct, but not enslave. It should allow for experimentation keeping in mind that all political systems have some meritorious features, and that no single class or group has the right of domination.

Turning to international problems, the author deplores the "realistic" solution of increasing the arms race which he believes leads our youth to gloominess and unrest. Because nuclear weapons threaten the destruction of everything built over the centuries, he urges a shift among nations from the "Wild West" posture of flaunting guns, to support for an international court and a multinational force which will enforce a universal international code of equity and integrity.

He is convinced that nationalism has become too narrow-minded and that there is a mutual benefit in supporting each other inasmuch as each nation possesses qualities which can benefit the others. The society of nations should come up with a plan to deal with poverty, crime, ignorance, and injustice on a global scale.

Cernuschi believes that the rivalry between the two superpowers is inherently dangerous. He therefore urges the development of a third power to balance the antagonism, specifically the United States of Europe toward which some progress has been made. He also recognizes that the concept of détente has been distorted by the Soviet Union to justify expansionism and repressionism, and urges us to redefine, presumably through negotiations, the meaning and the mutual obligations involved in détente. However valuable these immediate needs are, priority is given to the shifting of our resources from the production of armaments to common constructive endeavors.

His final hope for resolving the international confrontation is the elimination of its ideological base. In his judgment Adam Smith's capitalism has disappeared in the West into a type of cooperativism between owners, the state, and the workers. The other bloc is characterized by a state capitalism rather than communism. He hopes both sides will see that their ideologies are not as far apart as is usually assumed, and that they can cooperate on the basis of "a new intermediate social system acceptable to both."

Whether the vision of *The Constructive Manifesto* is a feasible one is surely open to debate. Certainly there are significant economic and political obstacles to many of these ideas. It is a formidable task to reduce arms, to create an effective international court, to come up with a common plan to deal with world poverty, to get East and West to agree on any kind of social system, or even to create a United Europe. Nevertheless, no step toward worthwhile long range goals can be taken unless they are first forcefully and appealingly stated. Cernuschi's book provides a stimulating contribution toward a more comprehensive vision in an era in which many thinkers are merely trying to solve our immediate problems.

                              Ralph C. Meyer, Ph.D.
                              Associate Professor of Political Science
                              Fordham University
                              College at Lincoln Center

# TABLE OF CONTENTS

|             | Preface ........................... 5<br>by Dr. Ralph C. Meyer |
|---|---|
| Chapter I   | Bourgeoisie and Communism .......... 13 |
| Chapter II  | Was Marx Always Right in His<br>Assessments and Predictions? .......... 21 |
| Chapter III | How Marxism in Practice Distorted<br>Its Own Ideological Principles ......... 37 |
| Chapter IV  | The Human Profile of Karl Marx ....... 47 |
| Chapter V   | The Obsolescence of the Marxist<br>Concept ........................... 63 |
| Chapter VI  | The Actual Yearning for a Truly<br>Revolutionary Breakthrough .......... 79 |
| Chapter VII | The Constructive Manifesto ........... 87 |

CHAPTER I

# Bourgeoisie and Communism

One hundred and thirty years have passed since the *Communist Manifesto* was published, and it is difficult to believe that nearly two billion people still regard it as the most up-to-date model for shaping their lifestyles. It may seem that, for them, time was brought to a standstill and nothing happened or changed within nearly one and a half centuries. The truth is that the period between the middle of the nineteenth century and the end of the twentieth century witnessed the most dramatic change in human conditions in history.

Let's have a look from our present perspective back to 1848 and analyze Marx's and Engel's theories. We are probably in an objective enough position to clear up some very widespread misunderstandings.

It is widely accepted that Marx was the one who established the theoretical basis for a communist order. He was supposedly the one who coined the phrase *communism* and predicted that our society must inevitably evolve into a communist system.

The truth is that scientific research has made even more clear what was already admitted by Engels: that Haxthausen, Georg Ludwig von Maurer, Thomas Hunt Morgan and others established that prehistoric tribal societies practiced a common ownership of land. The first officially designated commune was an association of the bourgeois (or burgers), so violently hated by Marx, who as early as in the Middle Ages obtained the right to govern themselves.

The appropriation of the name *communism* was necessary for Marx to distinguish his ideology from that of the socialists whom he despised, calling their theoreticians "dirty Jews of Negro blood"[1] and stigmatizing all other socialist groups outside his Feudal Socialism with names like: *Petty-Bourgeois Socialism, German "True" Socialism, Conservative or Bourgeois Socialism, or Critical Utopian Socialism.*[2]

All socialist parties — according to him — were not serving the interests of the working class, but those of its enemies. Marx coined the name for the workers, *proletarians*, as ancient Romans called paupers; and, according to Marx, the enemy number one of the working class was the bourgeoisie or the presently called upper middle class.

At the same time that the bourgeoisie was violently hated and vilified by Marx, he was unable to liberate himself from admiring and praising it. In the first chapter of the *Communist Manifesto* Marx had intended to prove how disastrous a role the bourgeoisie played in history, but concurrently he was unable to avoid giving it credit for many achievements. In spite of making clear his position as an unequivocal enemy of the bourgeoisie, many of his accusations sounded like eulogies. Today many communist states have already been established — based on Marx's theories. But, paradoxically, all the evils ascribed by Marx to the bourgeoisie can *more* easily be found in the totalitarian systems than in western democracies. Let's consider some excerpts from the first chapter of the Communist Manifesto, "Bourgeois and Proletarians," which are, in fact, an involuntary praise for the bourgeoisie.

"The bourgeoisie, historically, has played a most revolutionary part....

"It has pitilessly torn asunder the motley feudal ties that bound man to his "natural superiors...."

It has been the first to show what man's activity can bring about. It has accomplished wonders far surpassing Egyptian pyramids, Roman aqueducts, and Gothic cathedrals; it has conducted expeditions that put to shame all former Exoduses of nations and crusades....

"All fixed, fast-frozen relations, with their train of ancient and venerable prejudices and opinions are swept away, all new formed ones become antiquated before they can ossify....

"To the great chagrin of reactionaries it had drawn from under the feet of industry the national ground on which it stood....

"In place of the old local and national seclusion and self-sufficiency, we have intercourse in every direction, universal inter-dependence of nations. And as in material, so also in intellectual production. The intellectual creations of individual nations become common property. National one-sidedness and narrow-mindedness become more and more impossible, and from the numerous national and local literatures, there emerges a world literature....

"The bourgeoisie, by rapid improvement of all instruments of production, by the immensely facilitated means of communication, draws all, even the most backward nations, into civilization....

"The bourgeoisie, during its rule of scarcely one hundred years, has created more massive and more colossal productive forces than have all preceding generations together....

"Subjection of Nature's forces to man, machinery, application of chemistry to industry and agriculture, steam-navigation, railways, electric telegraph, clearing of whole continents for cultivation, canalization of rivers, whole populations conjured out of the ground — what earlier century had even a presentiment that such productive forces slumbered in the lap of social labor?...

"The less the skill and exertion of strength [applied] in manual labor, in other words when modern industry becomes developed to relieve it, the more is the labor of men superseded by that of women....

It sees itself compelled to appeal to the proletariat, to ask for its help, and thus to drag it into the political arena. The bourgeoisie itself, therefore, supplies the proletariat with its own elements of political and general education...."[3]

Of course, all these characteristics of the bourgeoisie are evidently wrong and harmful in Marx's opinion, but the only explanation of why they are so evil is that they were originated and achieved by the bourgeoisie and not by the proletariat. Another series of wrongdoings enumerated in the same chapter ironically very much resemble features of the totalitarian state:

"It has drowned the most *heavenly* [italics author's] *ecstasies of religious fervor*, of chivalrous enthusiasm, of philistine sentimentalism, in the icy water of egoistical calculation....

"The bourgeoisie had stripped of its halo every occupation hitherto honored and looked up to with reverent awe. It has converted the physician, the lawyer, *the priest* [italics author's], *the poet, the man of science* into its paid wage laborers....

"The bourgeoisie has torn away from the family its sentimental veil....

"The need of a constantly expanding market for its product [read propaganda] chases the bourgeoisie [the USSR] over the whole surface of the globe. It must nestle everywhere, establish connections everywhere....

"[It] Has concentrated property in a few hands. [Single owner — the state — in a communist system.] The necessary consequence of this was political centralization [in the Kremlin]. Independent, or but loosely connected provinces, with separate interests, laws, governments, and systems of taxation became lumped together into one nation, with one government, one code of laws, one national class-interest, one frontier, and one customs-tariff [as in the USSR]....

"The cost of production of a workman is restricted, almost entirely, to the means of subsistence that he requires for his maintenance, and for propagation of his race.... [Compare wages and living standard of the working class of the U.S.A. with that of communist countries.]

"As the use of machinery and division of labor increases, in the same proportion the burden of toil also increases, whether by prolongation of the working hours, by increase of the work exacted in a given time or by increased speed of the machinery, etc...."

The present-day Soviet laborer has an obligatory minimum quantity of work — called *norma* — to perform. In order to motivate him to surpass this already high requirement, and produce more, he is continuously incited by two methods. One is the so-called "socialist competition," consisting of the practice of challenging one group of workers or an entire plant by another group or factory with the same specialty, to compete in achieving a larger output. The second method consists of creating a distinctive elite of workers who surpass the *norma*, calling them *Stakhanovtcy*. The name was created by glorifying a miner named Stakhanov who extracted thirty times more coal than his companions.[4]

"Masses of laborers, crowded into the factory, are organized like soldiers. As privates of the industrial army they are placed under the command of a perfect hierarchy of officers and sergeants. Not only are they slaves of the bourgeois class, and of the bourgeois state; they are daily and hourly enslaved by the machine, by the foreman, and above all, by the individual bourgeois manufacturer himself...."[5]

The Marxist countries have not only copied their industrial methods from the capitalist system, but deprived the workers of the right to fight back through strikes and collective bargaining. The bureaucratic apparatus has been enlarged and strengthened. Discipline has been tightened in all Marxist countries to such a point that a worker being late more than three times risks not only dismissal but also prosecution. The pay is much lower than in the capitalist system and workers' standard of living is much inferior. Ownership of a car, house, refrigerator, air conditioning, dishwasher, washing machine, or stereo belongs to the sphere of unattainable dreams; and in many remote geographical areas even their existence is unknown. Besides technical and administrative hierarchy, the factories have a political instructor — *politruk* — and all workers are obliged to endure constant political indoctrination through boring speeches and dull courses. In addition, the security officer's task includes political surveillance and disclosure of possible dissidents. In any conversation, criticizing remarks are carefully avoided, as they can be considered a serious offense labeled "the slandering of the state."

The low salary is further reduced by "voluntary" contributions in cash and additional work hours for the benefit of activities and organizations sponsored by the government.

"The 'ragged proletariat'[6] the social scum, that passively rotting mass thrown off by the lowest layers of old society, may, here and there, be swept into the movement by a proletarian revolution; its conditions of life, however, prepare it far more for the part of a bribed tool of reactionary intrigue."[7]

The last sentence describes exactly the opposite of what is really happening. The spiteful labeling of the less privileged and despised class has no justification at all. In today's panorama of the classification "ragged proletariat" will fall the slum dweller, the unemployed youth — especially black and Hispanic — and, on the international level, citizens of all underdeveloped countries; and, in Western Europe, the foreign workers coming from Italy, Yugoslavia, Portugal, Turkey, and Algeria to work in France, Germany, Switzerland, and the Scandinavian countries. They are either filling the temporary shortage of labor in moments of high prosperity and dismissed during periods of recession, or performing the repulsive jobs, which the natives don't want. They are usually paid less than the national, strongly unionized workers, and they can not afford the expensive rents for decent quarters.

The people in all these unfortunate categories were not "occasionally swept into a proletarian revolution," as Marx predicted, even though the capitalist system was unable, or unwilling, to resolve thoroughly their situation.

Marx's remark that their conditions of life prepare them for being a "bribed tool of intrigue" might be true, but certainly not in favor of the reactionaries, as Marx explained. What we have observed in many countries is that these people have been easily influenced by the extreme left.

> "The condition for capital is wage labor. Wage labor rests exclusively on competition between the laborers."[8] [Communism has not, however, abolished the wage system but reinforced it by "socialist competition."]
>
> "The modern bourgeois society that has sprouted from the ruins of feudal society has not done away with class antagonisms. It has only established new classes, new conditions of oppression, new forms of struggle in place of the old ones."[9]

The above is, of course, a perfect description of the actual situation in a communist regime. The old privileged class has been annihilated to cede place to the omnipotent bureaucracy, which enjoys all possible advantages and privileges. The new conditions of oppression are widely known and supersede in perfidy the old ones. The underground struggle of the dissidents and their pitiless persecution bears a striking similarity to the situation of the revolutionaries before 1917.

1. Francis B. Randall, *Marx the Romantic.*
2. Statement made in 1848.
3. Karl Marx and Friedrich Engels, *The Communist Manifesto*, Part III.
4. For more details about how the *Stakhanovtcy* system has been created, see: Alberto Cernuschi's *Life and Voyages of Century.*
5. Marx and Engels, *The Communist Manifesto*, Chapter 1.
6. "Lumpenproletariat" in original; a deprecatory term for the unskilled and permanently unemployed.
7. Marx and Engels, *op. cit.*
8. Ibid.
9. Ibid.

## CHAPTER II

# Was Marx Always Right in His Assessments and Predictions?

"A specter is haunting Europe — the specter of communism."[1]

Absolutely true. But in a completely different sense than that conveyed by Marx. He depicted the communist party as nascent power, in need of self-confidence, organization, and heralding to the whole world its views, aims and intentions. It was then a party persecuted by the "holy alliance to hunt down and exorcise the specter: Pope and Tsar, Metternich and Guizot, French radicals and German police-spies." But the situation has changed. Communism is no more the weakling and today nobody doubts its power. The specter haunting the Western World is precisely this continuously growing power. This causes anxiety about what will happen to the West if this power overtakes the remaining part of the world not already under its control. The bombastic and idealistic slogans of communism have been contradicted by the continuous piling up of facts. After being in power for more than sixty years, the Communists have given the world a clear picture of what can be expected if their strategy succeeds and the entire world is ruled by the Kremlin.

The specter that is haunting the Eastern Communist nations is that of Eurocommunism, which deviates so much from the Eastern guidelines. By admitting the plural party system and its fierce opposition to Moscow's hegemony and domination, Eurocommunism has broken the old tradition that all Communist movements around the world must be unquestioningly directed from Moscow.

The first major cleavage in the Communist monolith appeared in 1948 when Tito refused to be bossed, directed and remote controlled by Stalin. The Communist nations and the West witnessed, not only his survival, but his complete rehabilitation in the eyes of the Kremlin. During the first outburst of rage by the Kremlin, Tito was excommunicated, labeled traitor to the working class and a lackey of the imperialists and capitalists. Yet Tito remained beyond intimidation. Taking the well-calculated risk that Moscow would not dare to use military intervention to settle an ideological rift, Tito was within several years finally received in Moscow with all the honors of a friendly leader and ally.

The next renegade was Mao, who after 1949 never counted on Stalin's approval in his astute strategy to defeat Chiang Kai-shek, Mao finally established himself as the Communist leader of China (except for Formosa) and created a rival ideological breed of communism. Not only did Mao defy Moscow, but he openly declared Chinese hostility to the Russians, a policy prevailing until the present day.

Encouraged by the evident impunity toward heretics to the Kremlin pope (the party secretary), more voices have been raised in the Communist camp, for an individual interpretation of Marxism, more suitable for other nations than the Russian version. Eurocommunism — in spite of Moscow's acute allergic reaction — was finally legalized at the 20th Soviet Party Congress in 1956, when Khrushchev was obliged to admit publicly that revolution could be achieved in a different way than in the Bolshevik pattern of 1917-18. Since then Eurocommunism has been the *enfant terrible* of the Communist hardliners, daring to abolish such holy commandments as "dictatorship of the proletariat" and admitting (at least in promise) the existence of a multiparty system and opposition to government.

"The history of all hitherto existing society is the history of class struggle."[2]

Only partially true. While many historical developments — either peaceful or by war — have been motivated by economic factors, there have been many that had ideological or religious backgrounds.

Marx asserted that the structure of an ancient society was more complicated than that of a modern society, in which the class antagonism had been increased. He said:

> "In the earlier epochs of history, we find almost everywhere a complicated arrangement of society into various orders, a manifold gradation of social rank. In ancient Rome we had patricians, knights, plebeians, slaves; in the Middle Ages, feudal lords, vassals, guildmasters, journeymen, apprentices, serfs; and in almost all of these particular classes, again, other subordinate gradations.
>
> "Our epoch, the epoch of the bourgeoisie, shows, however, this distinctive feature: it has simplified the class antagonisms.
>
> "Society as a whole is more and more splitting up into great hostile camps, into two great classes directly facing each other: *bourgeoisie* and *proletariat*."[3]

Completely false. Just the basic statement that the organization of an ancient society was more complicated than that of a contemporary society cannot be upheld by anybody even superficially acquainted with sociology. Not only does the structure of present-day society become constantly more intricate, but through the affinity, or contrast of interests, new, strange and paradoxical alliances are constantly emerging.

Consider, for example, the military establishment. The usual argument used by the critics of the inflated defense budget is that the industry involved in fulfilling contracts has an interest in creating the hysteria of imminent danger, to secure its source of income. According to Marx, the "proletariat," that is, the workers in this industry, should be in hostile opposition and have completely different objectives than the management. The reality is in a sharp contrast with Marx's depiction.

First, the specialized, highly trained and well-paid worker in the defense industry has nothing in common with the down-and-out pauper-proletarian of the *Communist Manifesto*. With his own house, two cars and a savings account, he could be more easily identified with Marx's bourgeois. His interests are tied not to inflammatory "worker against the tycoon" but to the industry assuring his income and prosperity. He doesn't give a damn about any pacifistic tendencies, and is more than happy when the production of artifacts of destruction is at its peak.

In the Communist bloc, the contradiction with Marx is even more blunt. The government, which supposedly represents the working class, should be theoretically the very image of pacifism. But the Communist military establishment has succeeded in gaining a highly privileged position, and is not interested in losing it through a disarmament policy. The vicious circle of threats, fear, and the arms race is equally strengthened in the West and the East by the far-flung interests of all personally involved in the military machine.

Marx explained how the bourgeoisie gained in power at the expense of society's other strata.

> "Modern industry has established the world market, for which the discovery of America paved the way. This market has given an immense development to commerce, to navigation, to *communication by land* [author's italics]. This development has, in its turn, reacted on the extension of industry; and in proportion as industry, commerce, navigation, railways extended, in the same proportion the bourgeoisie developed, increased its capital,

and pushed into the background *every class* [author's italics] handed down from the Middle Ages."[4]

The first striking impression is that Marx's entire description is anachronistic. Not only do the phrases "communication by land" and "railways extended" seem behind time, but the simplicity of reducing the complex modern society to two classes is a puerile image of the real sociological structure in today's world.

Marx's conclusion that the bourgeoisie, the directing upper-middle class, was pushing into the background every other class, was pronounced a half a century before Ford and other American industrialists realized that a well-paid labor force creates an additional mass of consumers for their products. Without any motivating humanitarian or altruistic reasons, Marx's "proletarians" evolved into a relatively affluent middle class, under the protection of continuously stronger and more demanding unions. Together with this transformation, a new class of technocrats has been pushed forward and not backward: engineers, mechanics, economists, planners, accountants, advertisers, finance and organization experts.

"The bourgeoisie has at last, since the establishment of modern industry and of the world market, conquered for itself, in the modern representative state, exclusive political sway. The executive of the modern state is but a committee for managing the common affairs of the whole bourgeoisie."[5]

A beautiful phrase for a demagogic speech. Bombastic words intended to easily inflame discontented masses. But are the masses discontent?

Marx's clear division of all society into two opposite blocs — the bourgeoisie, flooded with all kinds of privileges and advantages, on one side, and the exploited, miserable, starving proletariat on the other — is obsolete in heavily industrialized nations. With the rapidly evolving changes of the space age new forms of society and different strata have emerged. As we distinguish among nations, powers and superpowers, so we have the rich, super-rich, giant trusts and monopolies, international conglomerates and banks, with all the intermediate nuances of large, middle-sized and small corporations. Their employees form a likewise enormous diversity: on the top of the ladder, majority shareholders and top executives, drawing high six-figure salaries plus bonuses; in the middle, directors, engineers, foremen, highly skilled labor; and on the bottom, the porters and cleaning women. But all along the ladder the starving exploited "proletarian" is absent. It is true that the competition is hard, and the availability of labor greater than the demand, with consequent unemployment, but at the same time we witness numerous individuals "making it" — men and women succeeding in climbing from the bottom to the top of the ladder.

False and anachronistic is Marx's assertion that "the executive of the modern state is but a committee for managing the common affairs of the whole bourgeoisie." We are not blind and brainwashed, but see clearly the strong lobbying for the interests of the overprivileged. Yet at the same time, perhaps not so much for principles and morality as for the advancement of personal careers, we view powerful union action, consumer protection agencies, and — unfortunately insufficient — initiative to alleviate the conditions of the underprivileged. Fewer laws are enacted to reinforce the prosperity of the well-off than to trim their privileges in favor of the less fortunate. The prolonged coalminers' strike in the winter of 1978 demonstrated that even the intervention of the courts and the President of the United States was powerless against the determined will of labor to improve its condition. In the conflict of interest between employees and employers, it is not always the employers who have the upper hand.

> "In place of the numberless indefeasible chartered freedoms, [the bourgeoisie] has set up that single, unconscionable freedom — free trade. In one word, for ex-

ploitation, veiled by the religious and political illusions, it has substituted naked, shameless, direct, brutal exploitation."[6]

What a perfect description of a typical Communist totalitarian state, and an example of an incoherent demagogic, senseless accumulation of strong words, without any logical argumentation. No wonder that Marxism is now looking for followers in the most remote spots of the globe, with the highest ratio of illiteracy and, consequently, lowest access to objective information.

In 1848 Marx explained in the following way the economic fluctuations in a capitalist system.

"It is enough to mention the commercial crises that by their periodical return put on trial, each time more threateningly, the existence of the entire bourgeois society. In these crises a great part not only of the existing products, but also of the previously created productive forces, are periodically destroyed. In these crises there breaks out an epidemic that, in all earlier epochs, would have seemed an absurdity — the epidemic of over-production. Society suddenly finds itself put back into a state of momentary barbarism; it appears as if a famine, a universal war of devastation had cut off the supply of every means of subsistence; industry and commerce seem to be destroyed; and why? Because there is too much civilization, too much means of subsistence, too much industry, too much commerce."[7]

If in 1848 there was already too much civilization, industry and commerce, what would the venerable prophet of universal happiness say about the present fantastic and continuously accelerating race of technological prodigy? The simplistic explanation of economic crises by overproduction seems to ignore Adam Smith's principle of automatic regulation based on offer and demand, competition and free initiative. Besides, after more than six decades of functioning, the Marxist economic rule, with its chronic scarcity and inadequate supply of goods, cannot pretend to be superior or more efficient than the overproduction of a free system.

The bleak prophecies by Marx for the capitalist system have also proved erroneous.

> "The productive forces at the disposal of society no longer tend to further the development of the conditions of bourgeois property; on the contrary, they have become too powerful for these conditions, by which they are fettered, and so soon as they overcome these fetters, they bring disorder into the whole of bourgeois society, endanger the existence of bourgeois property. *The conditions of bourgeois society are too narrow to compromise the wealth created by them* [author's italics]."[8]

The last sentence is particularly ironic when a general comparison of wealth is made between the East and West. The Communist propaganda pretends that the Eastern worker is completely unaware of the enormous difference between his own standard of living and that of his Western counterpart. Owning a spacious house, with two cars, stereo, color TV, and sometimes a piano is an unimaginable dream, possible only — according to the propaganda — for the capitalist tycoons, exploiting pitilessly the oppressed and enslaved working class. The ratio of productivity of rural workers per capita is 1 to 13.6 in favor of U.S. in the production of grain and 1 to 12.6 in meat. About 33 million Soviet farmers, one fourth of the total work force, produced in the 1979 season 179 million tons of grain, 15.3 million tons of meat. Grain in 1980 recovered slightly to 189.2 million tons, but output in 1981 was so poor that it was not made public. Soviet and Western agricultural experts estimated it below 160 million tons.

Just 4 million U.S. farmers, less than one-twentieth of all workers, turned out 295 million tons of grain and 22.7 million tons of meat. On the industrial side the U.S.S.R. is far behind schedule continuously.

The most flowery slogans of Communist propaganda cannot substitute for the psychological incentive of private initiative, when individuals are working for themselves.

The Soviet system cannot openly admit a complete fiasco, but there is already a push for increased emphasis on private rural plots, based on experiments in Latvia and Georgia.

How strange it seems that Soviet authorities still remain blind and cannot learn from their own statistics, which admit that private-plot farmers use only 1.4 percent of the Soviet Union's farmland, but produce 61 percent of its potatoes, 54 percent of its fruit, 34.3 percent of its eggs, 30.2 percent of its vegetables and 29 percent of its meat and milk.

Tsarist Russia was an important exporter of grain, in times when the most primitive utensiles and agricultural methods were used. Today the highly mechanized U.S.S.R., with the help of chemical fertilizers, is unable to feed itself, and depends on massive acquisitions of grain abroad.

Another reflection upon Marxist economy is the fact that the majority of Communist countries are heavily indebted to Western governments and banks. The repayment of the capital when due, if not conveniently refinanced, might most certainly lead to default.

Endless are the examples that could be cited to indicate how wrong Marx was in frantically heralding the overwhelming economic superiority of his social system. In their book *Wage Labor and Capital,* Marx and Engels insisted:

> "The price of commodity is equal to its cost of production." Clarifying that, they stated: "The worker sells his labor power and not his labor."[9]

The assertion is too simplistic even for the nineteenth century, all the more so for today, when so many factors completely alien to the real cost of production play a predominant role in the fluctuation of prices. Availability of stockpiles, unexpected demands caused by political tensions, war fever, drop in sales as a consequence of recession, and similar determinants produce considerable ups and downs in the international markets. Besides these factors, market prices are also influenced by artificially created causes: waves of speculation, fashion trends, or by the media announcement of an imminent shortage or abundance of a certain commodity. Determinants regulating prices can be real, such as a good or poor harvest, or artificially manipulated by shadowy interests, not necessarily capitalist. The motivation to influence the rise or decline of prices may as well stem from a giant, international commodities trader aiming to cash in on an increased value of his inventory as from a Communist state, itself a buyer (of grain, for example) aiming to acquire the commodity more cheaply. It is evident that today's mechanisms of interchange are too complex to be expressed in a simplistic formula pronounced in a past century.

Policy and principles can be affected or changed by hundreds of known factors as well as by a completely new event. They can change as a result of a breakthrough in a new technology, or as a result of a political turmoil in a supplier country (Iran, for example). The quintupling of oil prices within a few years was caused by the creation of OPEC, a single political move without any relation to or influence by labor conditions.

In his analysis of three sources of income, Marx stated as undisputed truth that *"Capital* [author's italics] brings in profit for the capitalist, the *soil* [author's italics] brings in ground rents for the landowner, and *labor power* [author's italics] earns wages for the worker."[10] This could have been partially true in the time of private moneylenders and landed gentry. Today, loan sharks are on the margin of the law, and small capitalists, as well as large banks, are obliged to make their capital "work" to obtain profit. Great landholders, gambling away the money obtained from working tenants to whom they rented parcels of their vast estates, are a feature of the past.

Today's most common type of farmer in the Western countries is a hard-working owner of a small to medium-sized farm. In such an enterprise, the property — capital — is indivisibly united with labor to produce income. Even the common worker, whose unique source of income is his labor, is organized (in developing countries tries to get organized) in powerful unions, which protect his interests. These unions can function only as a result of the workers' financial contributions — capital — allowing the labor organization to maintain a costly bureaucratic machine of professionals, whose only specialty is to wrest out more privileges for the working class. The union machine is a pure capital investment, which yields profit in the form of greater benefits for the working class. In a modern society, capital and labor are no longer two opposed camps, engaged in a merciless fight, but two forces that willy-nilly are obliged to cooperate for a mutual benefit.

The entire problem is reduced to a just and equitable sharing of these benefits, and organized labor in the West can not complain that it is not getting and increasing its share in a fair participation. In the most advanced countries, such as Sweden, Great Britain, and the U.S., the accusations that the unions are abusing their power are already equalizing the reproaches that big capital is giving an inch and taking a mile.

The advantageous position of capital is still evident, and in the Third World, where labor is unorganized, the governments often corrupted and manipulated by selfish interests, the old-fashioned nineteenth-century Marxism still has a receptive ground.

Marx's basic division of costs of production into 1) the means of production (raw materials, etc.), 2) the ground rent, 3) wages,[11] is completely inadequate for modern production. It is sufficient to analyze any balance sheet of a small, medium or large manufacturer to establish that in addition to these three elements of cost we have depreciation, interest, and taxes, which alone average to amount to fifty percent of the net profit. Based on his erroneous premises, Marx engaged in a Talmudic logomachy, concluding that the rate of wages is determined by the wages themselves, and the price of commodities by the price of commodities! Furthermore, where does this puzzling conclusion lead?[12] To a confirmation of the capitalist theoretician Adam Smith's thesis that the market is auto-regulated, that capital (that is, production) will automatically direct itself where profit (that is, demand) is greatest, abandoning sectors with lower demands and profits.

Marx continued as if he were Smith's diligent disciple, explaining that the escape of capital from and diminished production of the unprofitable sector will self-regulate and reverse the situation, as the diminished availability will self-propel the demand, prices and profit. We don't need a better interpreter of the traditional capitalist dogma of non- interference and *laissez faire!*

Another point that Marx involuntarily accentuated in favor of a free enterprise was the efficiency of management which has an enormous influence in producing the profit. During his lifetime the inefficient management of socialist enterprises had not yet been experienced. So it is astonishing how his remarks could be applied in a comparison between the profitability of capitalist versus socialist enterprises. Marx stated:

> "As a matter of fact, we have invariably had to start, in our discussion, from the presumption that the management of the business is an efficient one. Much depends on the personal efficiency of the manager. Should the latter prove inefficient, the profit of any individual undertaking can easily sink below the general average rate, whereas a capable manager may succeed in raising it above the average."[13]

In citing excerpts from Marx's *Das Kapital* we don't intend to emphasize its importance from a scientific, or even Communist doctrinal point of view. *Das Kapital* is rarely read by the Communists, and not highly considered by Western specialists. Francis B. Randall in his *Marx the Romantic* said, "Economists, historians, and philosophers have long since ceased to take it as a serious contribution to their fields. It is so long and so dull a book that few Marxists can read or understand it."[14] As long ago as 1919, Julian Borchard had a similar opinion, noting: "The book is quite incomprehensible for the layman. Marx's manner of expressing himself is uncommonly difficult to grasp."

Our purpose in using extracts from this work is to analyze Marx's thoughts in the light of contemporary conditions and to try to determine objectively whether if we can, in some way, profit from his teaching and improve our way of life.

One of Marx's obsessions was the problem of profit. He was inclined to prove that capital (that is, money) takes a profit without adding any real value to the commodity. But is this the case? Marx, himself, had serious doubts about the subject. He asked:

> "But how can profit derive spontaneously from capital? For the production of any given commodity the capitalist needs a certain sum, say $25.00. In this sum are included all the costs of production, i.e. raw and auxiliary materials, wages, the wear of the machinery, tools, buildings, etc. He subsequently sells the finished commodity for $27.50. If we conclude that the finished commodity is really worth $27.50, we must necessarily conclude that this increased value, which has accrued during the process of production, has arisen out of nothing, seeing that all the values for which the capitalist has paid $25.00 existed previous to the existence of the commodity in question. The idea of something created out of nothing is unacceptable to human reason. Hence economists have

always held in the past, and still hold today, that the value of the commodity does not increase during the process of production, but that when this process is finished the capitalist has only in possession an object of the same value as previously — that is to say, in the case assumed by us, of the value of $25.00."[15]

How infantile and false is this reasoning! How unacceptable in the case of ultramodern industry, let us say, computers. The value of the raw materials, the metal and plastic, in a computer can be worth $150.00, but the computer may sell for $500.00. The rest is not only labor's wages, but also compensation for the inventiveness, ingenuity and talent of those who conceived the project. The pay of salaried project engineers Marx would accept as part of the cost but not the "capitalist" part, that is, the wages of the management, which originated the idea. In his thinking, the ownership always adds a profit for "nothing!"

Marx's prejudicial approach consists of a different evaluation of the intellectual value of the salaried engineers and of the value of "capitalist" management. In most cases the salaried engineers are only executing and elaborating on the directives conceived by the capitalist management, which made possible the enterprise to begin with.

We can not agree that "capital's" and management's merit is nil and its position parasitic, as even in Communist countries the directors are better paid than the lower echelon workers. In today's intricate financial world, large enterprises exclusively owned by an individual or a family are a rarity. Usually the original founder of the company was not only a phenomenon of ingenuity and drive, but also an exceptionally hard-working individual. The pure capitalist, who simply invests in shares of stock or who owns a part of the entire enterprise without being actively involved in it, through his confidence in the profitability of the venture, makes possible its creation by the founder, and its enlargement by the heirs. In

addition to these merits, capital, as such, has an interest value even in the Communist bloc, as its countries pay interest on loans received and charge interest for those it allots.
Endless are the mistakes and false assertions considered as a base of the Communist holy books.

1. Karl Marx and Friedrich Engels, Preface to *The Communist Manifesto*.
2. Ibid., Chapter 1.
3. Ibid.
4. Ibid.
5. Ibid.
6. Ibid.
7. Ibid.
8. Ibid.
9. Karl Marx and Friedrich Engels, *Wage Labor and Capital*. Original edition published in 1891. English translation published in 1951 in Moscow.
10. Karl Marx, *Das Kapital*, Volume III, German edition.
11. Ibid., Volume III, Part 1 and Part 2.
12. Ibid., Volume III.
13. Ibid.
14. Randall, *op. cit.*
15. Marx, *op. cit.* Volume III.

CHAPTER III

# How Marxism in Practice Distorted Its Own Ideological Principles

Let us consider for a while what the application of a communist order was supposed to bring to mankind and what it actually brought.

Among the innumerable socio-political systems of the past and present, all, without distinction of the variety of their appellations, heralded forth that their only and final objective was to make the masses happy. The variety of their names doesn't hinder us from dividing them all into two main groups: those in which the governing authority "knows best" what is good for the people, and enforces its policy, with more or less cruelty; and those in which the authority does not claim to be empowered by a divine, or any other superior, inspiration but struggles together with the people to resolve their most crucial problems.

Marx's communism was conceived under the influence of the Prussian imperial environment where enough power was left in the hands of the monarchy to permit it to do practically whatever it pleased; and first applied in the transition from a tzarist empire, which had no constitution at all. The more subdued the masses were under the tzar the more they aspired to genuine liberty as well as to improvement of their living conditions. What happened in reality in the transition of power from the tzars and monarchs to the Soviets and the revolutionary committees? The authority empowering the imperial house through the "grace of God" was transferred to the representatives of the "party," which also knew best how to make happy the masses.

It has long been known what happens to anybody who disagrees with this system for achieving happiness. In spite of, and contrary to, the genuine aspirations and hopes of the masses, the communist order puts itself in the same camp of all oppressive and dictatorial regimes.

Marx often cited examples of capitalist greediness in exploiting the working class without any scruples. His statistics were based on figures from the 1850s and 1860s.[1] The oppressive labor conditions he described have long ago ceased to exist, for the most part, in Western countries; but a certain similarity between his description of the tendency to prolong working hours can still be found today in the industries of communist systems.

Marx's accusation that "machinery instead of shortening the working time required for the production of a commodity becomes, in the hands of capital, the most powerful means for lengthening the working day beyond all bounds set by human nature"[2] is inaccurate today when workers' conditions are strictly controlled by unions. But those who are familiar with the atmosphere in the factories behind the Iron Curtain know how often "voluntary" and "spontaneous" decisions to prolong the working hours of laborers are applied. The practice of "socialist competition" systematically uses the method of challenging a workers' team in one factory with a team in another factory to increase productivity. This practice puts a constant pressure on the worker to produce more and work longer hours.

Often we hear a phrase such as, "If Marx were to rise from his grave and see what has been done to his doctrine, he would prefer to return quickly to his tomb, rather than witness the reality." There is a lot of truth in this ironical statement. We have sufficient grounds for believing that many of his expectations have not been fulfilled. Too many of his idealistic prophecies have failed to materialize to enumerate them all in this chapter.

Consider, for example, his concept of universality. Marx believed that "the working men have no country."[3] "The supremacy of the proletariat will cause to vanish national differences and antagonisms between people."[4] "The exploitation of one nation by another will be put to an end."[5] The reality has been quite different. Nationalism is strongly accented in the Soviet Union; and the evidently dominating role of the Russian nation, not only in the U.S.S.R., but in the satellite countries, is more than evident. All revolutions that have taken place in countries since Marx proclaimed his theories have had strongly nationalistic overtones. The educational background of the leaders of these revolutions has not been comparable to that of universally thinking working men, but rather to that of patriotic-minded bourgeois liberals.

"Proletarians of all countries unite!"[6] — Marx's bombastic slogan — was from the publicity point of view an excellent selling device, but nobody has been acting according to it. Always and everywhere, the revolutionary forces have been driven by their leaders on the fuel of national independence and chauvinistic ascendancy. Never have common interests and fraternity with those on the other side of the border been invoked; but, on the contrary, hostility and hatred for those professing opposing systems have been promoted.

Not only have workers from different countries never united in a common revolution, but socialist and communist governments have without minimal scruples massacred their own workers. Oppressive colonial methods, practiced by the British in India, the French in Algeria, the Belgians in the Congo, were taken over by Stalin in the Soviet Union, Jaruzelski in Poland, Hussak in Czechoslovakia, Kadar in Hungary, Mao in China, and other supreme leaders in Asia, Africa and wherever the revolution took power. No traces have appeared whatsoever of Engels's prediction: "The eternal union of the proletarians of all countries is still alive and lives stronger than ever."[7] On the contrary, international conventions of labor unions and other organizations have only covered up with their superficiality the disparate interests and policies of the workers' groups of various nations.

And what about individual freedom? According to Marx,

> "Once the communist system will be introduced, the antagonism of classes and the classes themselves will be abolished, and the proletariat will renounce its own supremacy. In place of the old bourgeois society with its classes and class antagonisms, we shall have an association in which *the free development of each is the condition for the free development of all.*"[8] [Italics author's.]

The reality of how the "free development of each" is practiced in communist nations is well known, and its description is rather superfluous.

Nevertheless, some excerpts from a secret manifesto of the first organized opposition in East Germany against the "Dictatorship of a Single Party" might be helpful. The document was first published by the magazine *Der Spiegel* (Nos. 1 and 2, 1978). As reprisal for this publication the offices of the magazine in East Germany were closed and its personnel expelled. As the magazine quoted the manifesto,

> "It is our objective to influence in all Germany a communist democratic order where all human rights of every citizen are realized, and according to the word of Marx, to destroy all conditions where man is an oppressed, despised and enslaved being. We don't believe in Father Marx, his son Jesus-Engels and Holy Spirit-Lenin, but if they were alive today, they would look with horror at the dogmatic, paganish, idolatory images made of themselves, and they would without doubt defect to the West to be able to freely express their ideas."

From the ideological point of view, these East German

rebels consider communism as a link in the long chain of thinking from Thomas More and Campanella through the French, English and German utopianists, and the Enlightenment, to the Socialist classics including Bebel, Rosa Luxemburg and Liebknecht. They also emphasize that the works of these last two communist fighters are not publicized in East Germany because these two Socialists advocated a pluralistic communism that should be based on a rational analysis and not on pure faith. According to these two all social changes should be based on a commitment to justice inspired by combative humanism. In opposition to "revisionist" communism the East German rebels called directly for an underground fight against the party's authorities. Conspiratorial methods practiced against the Nazi reign should, they believed, be used now in a restless struggle for the right of free expression and exchange of ideas. The mighty Soviet war machine they sharply criticized from the ideological point of view. The communist infiltration in African and Arab countries through supply of arms, personnel and training is labeled a "Colonial System" and "Red Imperialism." The militarization of the entire public life in the Eastern bloc is considered by the same rebel manifesto an enormous danger to world peace.

Further along in this underground manifesto, astonishment is expressed concerning Russian greed for land in a country that already holds such vast areas. Russia's quarrel with Japan over the tiny Kuril Islands is described as a great power's chauvinism in Asia.

The Soviet Union accepted détente because it could, through limited cooperation with the West, economically and technologically improve its backward position. The U.S.S.R. has benefited from the scientific cooperation and bilateral agreements of technical exchange, by using Western technology to tune up its military machine, aiming to be superior to the Western powers. A similar attitude was adopted, without the necessity of engaging in détente, during the Cold War era.

There is no other alternative — in the opinion of the rebellious East German communists — than the passage from the Asiatic method of production by state-capitalism into a real socialist society.

Why is there such a discrepancy between the promised paradise of the working class and the real situation behind the Berlin wall? The industrial and agricultural worker, after being stuffed to the point of nausea with blabber glorifying his highly privileged position, has only to look around and notice that the management class lives far better. No wonder that the worker's aspiration is to imitate them. Despite the propaganda of the press, radio, and TV, the worker knows well that the standard of living of the Western worker is much higher. Whom can he blame for the difference if not the bosses of the party? As the continual promises to relieve the distressing shortages of all kinds of goods are never fulfilled, the working class in the Eastern bloc might well reach the conclusion that its exploitation has not changed much from the old times.

The luminaries of the communist ideology, including Marx, Engels, and Lenin, have all taken the opportunity to be publicized in the bourgeoise press, notwithstanding the fact that they preached the destruction of the existing social structure.

Where is the liberty of expressing even minor disagreement with the party's rule in a Communist state? Instead of publishing in an editor's column in the official paper, any dissenter must use the clandestine *samizdat* (self-publication) with the risk of arrest and harsh prison terms.

When Karl Marx was editor-in-chief of the *Rheinische Zeitung*, he proclaimed that the duty of the press was to reveal all the noxious aspects of the ruling order. Have we ever seen an article in the Communist official press criticizing any aspect of the current established Communist order or a high Communist official still in power?

Marx also proclaimed that all circumstances should be

destroyed in which man is an oppressed, disdained and enslaved being. How does it really look from inside the wall?

During the "Spring of Nations" when true liberalism was flourishing in Europe, the German newspaper *Kölnische Zeitung* on July 1, 1848, sharply criticized the "republican ultras":

> "The old system, which we fought for years, was characterized by two qualities. First, it thought it had a monopoly on wisdom; it regarded everyone who did not accept this wisdom as guilty of high treason. Second, it never believed in the purity of motives of its opponents, but assumed that selfishness, malice, etc. were involved.
>
> "And our current republican ultras? With their cries of reaction, those people who everywhere suspect treason against the people, selfishness, etc., who never regard their opponents as erring persons, but solely as conscious enemies of the good, of the people, of their freedom. Now, take a look at them. If they do not resemble the old system, as one basilisk egg the other, there is no longer any similarity in the world."

Can the same judgment not be made about today's Communist rulers?

The founding fathers of the communist order took good care to impress on it the distinguished mark of anti-colonialism, pacifism, and anti-imperialism. What about the current formidable armament race engaged in by the Soviet Army, Navy and Air Force? The systematic stirring up of agitation in Africa and Asia by the supplying of arms, training, and instruction, can only be considered as Red Imperialism. The militarization of the entire public life in the Eastern bloc is another aspect of the same phenomenon.

Stalin's excesses have been explained by the enthusiasts of the system as deviation from the orthodox communist line. But Stalinism was not a deviation; it was a thoroughly devised system for annihilating any trace of opposition to and criticism of the ruling powers. It is presently practiced all over the globe, whether it be the red-lacquered version in the communist countries, or the black variant of the fascist dictatorships. As the latest political fashion we have now the return of theocratic rule by the mullahs of Iran.

Marx taught that everything that motivates humans originates in their brains. But are we sure that the pontiffs of the Kremlin are putting accurate information in the minds of their followers? The cultural accumulation of all mankind has been disseminated through the free flow and exchange of ideas and opinions, and not by the phantasmal fear of any contradicting thought. The idealistic promises of the early years of communism to create "brotherly" ties among workers and nations have degenerated into a reactionary great power policy aiming only to impose its rule and influence in the most remote parts of the globe.

The politics of any great state have never been guided by idealistic premises. Opportunism, possible gains, national interest have been the motives for political moves and decisions. But what would be Marx's opinion about a communist state concluding a pact with a Nazi-fascist state leading to an attack on a neighboring country, and sharing the conquered land with the invader?[9]

It would require a separate book to describe all the flagrant abuses committed by the Soviet state in which the dream of giving power to the working class has supposedly been realized. Show trials leading to the extermination of the former revolutionary companions of Stalin and his circle, as well as forced labor camps and mental clinics for distinguished citizens, whose only crime was a different opinion from the official one, have created a ruling system of absolute, uncontrolled power. All traces of human and democratic considerations have been erased, bringing about a neofeudalism, much more omnipotent than the old system, which was obliged to share power with the church.

Rosa Luxemburg, Karl Liebknecht, August Bebel and other idealistic believers in true socialism certainly did not imagine that when the goal of their fight was achieved, an oppressive machinery, employing an entire army of informants, spies and brute force, would be necessary to suppress any opposing ideologies, or that a wall would be erected to prevent escape from "paradise."

1. Karl Marx, *Das Kapital*, Volume II.
2. Ibid.
3. Marx and Engels, *The Communist Manifesto*, Part II.
4. Ibid.
5. Ibid.
6. Marx and Engels, *The Communist Manifesto*, End of Part IV.
7. Marx and Engels, Preface to *The Communist Manifesto*, 1890.
8. Marx and Engels, *The Communist Manifesto*, Part II.
9. The famous Ribbentrop-Molotov pact, which permitted Hitler to invade Poland, triggering the Second World War. The Soviet Union occupied the eastern part of Poland, which she retains today.

## CHAPTER IV

# The Human Profile of Karl Marx

Marx has been regarded by his followers as prophet and apostle, by his opponents as demon and source of all possible evil; therefore, rarely have we had an opportunity to gain an objective, unimpassioned assay of the kind of man he really was.

The most common discussion pivots around his Jewishness. The antagonists gladly take up his heritage as a negative factor, playing the anti-Semitic role wherever it can strike a resonance. His defenders, in an unconscious complicity — as if it were necessary to deny his origins — affirm how unrelated he was to the Jewish community and culture. In reality, Karl Marx became Christian at the age of six, when his father, Heinrich, purely for career reasons, baptized the entire family, embracing the evangelical faith. It was a century before the racial theories of Hitler and his theoretician Rosenberg; and such a passage was sufficient to give Marx's family the recognition that the umbilical cord with Jewry had been definitely severed.

Karl Marx never felt he had anything in common with Jews, and often, consciously or unconsciously, emphasized his distance by insulting his opponents as "dirty Jews of Negro blood,"[1] an invective he employed against Ferdinand Lassalle, German socialist and trade union leader in the sixties of the nineteenth century. Today, the pronouncement of a similar epithet would be sufficient to stigmatize him as the worst kind of racist. But was Marx's lack of any identification with Judiasm so absolute?

Is it possible that the influence of many generations of rabbis, both from his father's and mother's side, was nonexistent? It is much easier to modify attitude and behavior than a deeply ingrained cultural pattern, resulting from an ancient heritage.

As a matter of fact Marx's entire manner of reasoning resembles more talmudic *pilpul* than rigorous Cartesian logic. It is not important that Marx never felt anything in common with a religion and culture whose ties had been severed by his family. In spite of the fact that Heinrich Marx was completely assimilated, even before he changed his faith, the thought patterns of Karl's mind still functioned similarly to those of his ancestors. What we have in mind is the particular technique of twisting and juggling arguments in favor of a thesis when the objective is to prove it at any cost. Instead of gathering facts and consequently reaching a conclusion that naturally derives from the accumulated evidence, dialectical materialism pronounces first a supposed truth and gradually builds around it an entire intricate structure of arguments to prove it.

Karl Marx's obstinate hatred for the bourgeoisie makes it hard to believe that this was exactly his own family's background. His father was a legal counsellor in the Prussian higher bureaucratic echelons, with a solid well-remunerated position. His mother, Henriette, came from a family of wealthy Christian merchants in Holland. Karl himself courted for many years and finally married Jenny von Westphalen, daughter of Ludwig von Westphalen, member of an old aristocratic family, related on her mother's side to the dukes of Argyle, so well known in Scotland. Karl himself was not entirely free of the snobbish appeal of his wife's maiden name and often encouraged her to specify in her letters her title: Mrs. Jenny Marx, born Baroness von Westphalen.

The young Marx was the most gifted of the family's eight

children and the most favored by his parents, who called him *Glückskind*, child of luck. His mother especially had a deep affection for him. Karl used this sentiment as excellent leverage any time he needed money. He didn't restrain himself — while he was a fugitive from Prussian justice in London — from threatening her that he would return and risk arrest if he did not receive from her a specified amount. Karell, as his mother spelled his name, was very adroit in taking advantage of the special weakness she felt for him. He even asked for and received during her lifetime advances on the inheritance he was to receive after her death. His father was not less fond of his son, whom he considered extremely talented. Nevertheless, Heinrich Marx was not blind to Karl's selfishness and absolute lack of affection and sensitivity. He considered him so egocentric and vainglorious that he often admonished him to have more heart and sentiment.

Another feature of the young Karl was his way of writing, using bombastic and highly elaborate expressions, which predominated over the presentation of a clear and rational development of an idea. Even in mature years his passion for strong words and magniloquence overshadowed the logic and strength of his argumentation. From his younger years an interior conflict had existed between his desire for a settled, prosperous career in law and his innate desire for glory and celebrity.

In his youth Karl had no interest in politics. His mind was more inclined toward abstract and literary activity than toward any practical or scientific endeavor. He started to study law in Bonn, but had no major predilection for legal study and failed to dedicate much time to learning it. No exception from any typical German student of the time, he was more occupied with drinking and duelling than with his academic program. An arrest at night for disorderly conduct in a state of complete intoxication is on his school record.[2] If we add to this behavior excessive spending, much over his father's generous allowance, it becomes clear why his university studies were interrupted and Karl returned to his parents' home in Trier.

At this point he started seriously to court Jenny von Westphalen. It was in a certain sense a "social climber's" undertaking. She was the beauty of the town, her family's background and position was higher than his own. But the brusque, haughty and arrogant young man changed completely when he obstinately undertook to conquer the attractive young woman. He became a romantic, gallant and charming suitor, adroitly using his intellect as one of the arms of assault.

Jenny, herself a highly intelligent woman, four years older than Karl, was attracted by his sparkling, erudite conversations. But marriage was impossible, because the aspirant had no stable position at all, let alone a promising and influential one. Still, Jenny was already vanquished and willing to wait, keeping secret from her family the informal engagement. Karl's father was extremely happy about his son's choice but worried about the practical aspects of their future. He already knew that a stabilized position wasn't attuned to Karl's nature, and he could already foresee that some hardship could be expected for the beautiful daughter of an affluent nobleman. A test separation was decided upon, and the young Marx went to Berlin to continue his studies and to define his career.

In consideration of Karl's former ill success in law, his father suggested a change, perhaps a trial in chemistry. But Karl undertook poetry, which was more than common in that highly romantic era, and developed his special admiration for the luminaries of the period: Goethe, Lord Byron, Shelley, Lamartine, and Heine. All his poetry was dedicated to his beloved Jenny, to whom he sent his works, *Books of Love* and *Books of Songs*, which she appreciated very much. Posterity cannot assess their literary worth, as they have been lost. The entire series might also have been a ruse to keep Jenny's interest in Karl alive and alert during the six years of separation and waiting.

But there is evidence that young Marx took his literary aspirations seriously and was encouraged by his father to follow that direction. Besides lyrics of love, he tried his hand at a satire, a novel, and a play, although he ignored the practical suggestion of his father to tint his writings with highly patriotic colors, gloryfying the role and leaders of Prussia.

The expected recognition evaded him, and Jenny was the single enthusiast of his literary talent. Ignored completely by the professional critics, Marx developed a sense of self-criticism, causing him to be continuously in doubt of his own talent and literary gift. This made him believe that he could better judge writings than be a writer, and he decided to become a literary critic himself. The difficulty was in finding a critical magazine willing to print his reviews about the creative abilities of others. He found none.

The next matter of interest to him was philosophy, then considered the German specialty. Still, Marx's intensive searchings for himself, which could also be interpreted as a vainglorious drive for fame and recognition, were all abortive, in this early stage of his life. The "philosophical period" gave birth to an essay about the philosophy of law, combining his new fancy with his former studies of law. He even tried his strength in the metaphysical field, drawing up what might be considered a new system in competition with the established and recognized philosophers, but to no avail.

Adding failure to failure, Marx attempted to master foreign languages, to discover with grief that he wasn't especially gifted at it. These continuous fiascos were too much for an ambitious and proud nature and completely shattered Karl. He collapsed morally and physically. Medical help was urgently needed. As a result a change of environment and activity was prescribed.

At this stage of his life Marx made a move that many biographers ignore and his enthusiastic admirers don't even suspect: He volunteered for enrollment in the Prussian army. Yes! The presumed "revolutionary hero," the personification of modern rebellion, progressive thinking and dissidence, volunteered for the Junkers' stronghold, the symbol of upper-class privilege, an arrogantly dominant caste. It is astonishing to imagine how different might be the pattern of the globe and twentieth century history if Karl Marx had not been dismissed from the Prussian army for poor health.

He probably had the beginnings of tuberculosis, coughing up blood, but overcame it later by intensive hiking and open-air exercises. In spite of this setback, a government career was still Marx's objective. Now he planned to become a judge and eventually a professor of law. It is remarkable that all these projects were based on integrating and reinforcing the establishment, not fighting it.

After continuous failures of all plans, Karl calmed down his literary ambition, burned all his finished and unfinished writings, and opted instead for reading. Digesting an immense number of volumes in a new infatuation to instruct himself, he rediscovered his former interest in philosophy.

It was no more than normal that he fell under the influence of a thinker who dominated the intellectual trend of the epoch: Hegel. It wasn't, however, love at the first sight, for in the beginning Karl's own dominating nature collided with the grandiosity of Hegel's vigorous thinking and its codification.

After the initial adversity, Karl returned to Hegelianism, conquered by its dialectic; and this marked the first time Marx became attracted to the radical branch of a philosophical school. Marx either did not study, or disregarded, the "official" paths of Hegel's teachings, in which the apotheosis of universal order was well suited to the conservative adversaries of violent innovations. Later in his life Marx was obliged to make some "adjustments" in Hegel's theory to get rid of God, who was omnipresent in the Hegelian system.

Marx joined the "Doctor's Club," a loose institution frequented by the younger and nonconformist Hegelians. In spite of Hegel's vigorous and disciplined mind, much of his philosophy was not clearly defined, and could be, not only differently, but also conversely interpreted. His exaltation of rationality was explained by the conservative circles in favor of the existing order as the best possible result of a long evolution. Consequently, protest, rebellion, and an outcry for change was irrational and unworthy of a higher intelligence.

The "Doctor's Club," on the contrary, grouped young, rebellious and impatient elements, and reversed the interpretation of rationality. Well versed in dialectic, they had a motto: If everything real was rational, so the system, which was irrational, was unreal and subject to change, which would improve human well-being. They, the young, would help to straighten out mankind's path and shake the established order. This kind of reasoning was more suitable for Karl's ideology or, most probably, for his innate tendency toward mental acrobatics in twisting an argument.

In a short time Marx acquired a certain prominence in this circle, due to both his acute spirit and ample spending. The latter habit was of deep concern to his aging and ailing father, whose resources were in decline. But Karl insisted on receiving his allowances even though he had abandoned his formal studies in the university.

The first time that Karl Marx's name appeared in print was when his friend from the Doctor's Club, Karl Friedrich Köppen, dedicated to Marx his monograph on Friedrich the Great. It is amazing that Köppen and Marx, both considering themselves rebels and nonconformists, could be united in their admiration for a despotic ruler, personifying the Prussian establishment. The explanation might be that they were fascinated by his highly enlightened and open-minded personality.

The members of the Doctor's Club were all typically bourgeois. They had good positions in teaching, practicing law, writing or directing newspapers and publishing houses. Even one of the most extreme radicals, Arnold Ruge, who had spent six years in prison for attacking the government, had not hesitated to marry a wealthy woman, to have the means to hire an editorial staff to publish his own paper.

During this period of his life, Marx's rebellious activity was rather chaotic. He mounted violent and virulent attacks on religion that were tantamount to a direct assault on the consecrated authority. Such an assault was logical and understandable, as during the 1830s a general revival of religious feeling was popular in Germany and supported by the state. As the state was a symbol of oppression to Marx, calling for a crusade to destroy faith in God could be interpreted as equivalent to fighting for progress and the defense of human rights.

Such an attitude might be justified while the Prussian state was flirting with the church. But in 1837 the Archbishop of Cologne, Klemens von Droste-Vishering, was arrested and confined in a military prison. He had pushed the church's interests too hard, disregarding the state and even existing agreements with it. In the scandalous confrontation and violent polemic, the young rebels, who as a rule attacked the church, found themselves on the side and defense of the state. The situation became more uncomfortable when Friedrich Wilhelm IV made wide concessions to the church. The alliance of the rebels with the Prussian state was called off and the king stigmatized as having kissed the Pope's shoes.

Marx and the entire group intensified their attacks on the church, and their public declarations synchronized with the publication of books deriding religion and the scriptures: David Friedrich Strass' *Life of Jesus*, Bruno Bauer's *Christ and the Bible*, and Ludwig Feuerbach's *Essence of Christianity*.

Marx became one of the outstanding figures in the Doctor's Club without having a Ph.D. degree,. Criticized by his colleagues, and probably urged on by the necessity of obtaining a professorship to secure a steady income, Karl made the necessary preparations. He didn't want to face the exams in Berlin University, known to be extremely tough; he ignored as well his friend Bauer's advice to take the exams in Bonn in a much less demanding university, and opted finally to settle the matter by mail. In the small state of Saxe-Weimar obtaining the coveted diploma was very easy. As a matter of fact, for a fee of twelve *thalers* Marx obtained his doctor's diploma.

Marx's next step was to get the desired professorship. He couldn't count on his qualifications as he had never published anything that could testify to his erudition. The solution might be a friendly recommendation. The only possibility was Bruno Bauer, who somehow had obtained the chair of theology at Bonn University. But Bauer's position was too precarious to be of any help.

Marx was unable to impress the Bonn faculty with his brilliant spirit; with his diploma, which did not have the essential academic regularity; nor with his nonexistent scholastic achievements. The Doctor's Club believed for a while that his nomination was imminent, but in reality it never arrived. Finally his hope disappeared when Bauer, his sponsor, was dismissed from his post.

Marx was deeply disappointed, feeling that he could no longer let his fiancée placidly wait for a stable source of income, which was so reluctant to arrive. Resentment and the desire for vengeance against so unjust a society had been gradually building in Marx's psyche. A society unable to recognize his greatness was only worth being destroyed. Marx's already exuberant personality was reinforced by this unchecked hatred, and acquired an irresistible magnetism, capable of attracting admirers and followers.

In no time he became the center of a group of young rebels believing in his vision and leadership. One of these was destined to have his name attached to Marx's forever. Friedrich

Engels had admired Marx even before he met him. He wrote poetic eulogies about Marx's titanic power, describing him as a kind of demiurge, gifted with unusual force and clearly predestined to change history. This obviously idolatrous admiration was a decisive factor, explaining why the autocratic Marx preferred Engels over Bruno Bauer, Moses Hess, and other highly talented friends, as his intimate collaborator and partner.

From the very beginning of their relationship Marx imposed his leading role, and that of Engels was secondary. Describing any major work on which they had collaborated, Engels was always certain to admit that the basic thought belonged solely and exclusively to Marx.[3] This kind of submissiveness suited Marx well and explains how, in spite of his bellicose character, their friendship and collaboration endured a lifetime.

Engels's family background was such that it would bar him today from applying for a job in any communist country, or at least put him on the list of suspected "enemies of the people." His father was a wealthy textile industrialist, owner of cotton spinning mills in Germany and England. In spite of a strict religious education, Engels's nonconformism came very early into the open. Neither he nor Marx had at that time a precise picture of what they wanted to accomplish and what kind of program they were following. But it became clear that it was not only religion and the church that they could combat, but the entire social system, based on aristocratic privileges, with its oppression, hypocrisy, and corruption.

An additional element might also be a factor that induced Marx to choose Engels as his closest collaborator and partner. Engels had the financial means that Marx lacked. Marx's father had grown old and ill and was unable to continue to support his already adult son. Engels's father, on the contrary, in spite of disagreement with his son's lifestyle and ideological objectives, never used money as leverage to enforce changes in Friedrich's revolutionary course. The senior Engels's lavish remittances allowed Marx and his partner to finance the publication and distribution of their propaganda.

The fact that Engels nearly always responded to Marx's financial needs was only one of the many ways in which he manifested devotion for his partner and mentor. Engels's feelings for Marx were a strange mixture of filial regard and motherly protection. In many manuscripts which he wrote, he did not hesitate to assign the authorship to Marx. When Marx made the family servant Helen Demuth pregnant, Engels declared himself the father of the illegitimate son, Freddy.

Engels's friendship was continuously of great service to Marx, from such banalities as finding a treatment for his carbuncles, which made it difficult for him to sit down and write, to using his own multiple talents and reputation to advance their political goals.

Friedrich Engels was already well known under the pseudonym of Friedrich Oswald for his inflamatory articles published in the German antireactionary newspaper *Telegraph für Deutchland,* and once his real identity was discovered, Marx had no difficulty in having him admitted to the revolutionary circle of young Hegelians. Marx appreciated and made good use of Engels's writing talent, as his style was much clearer than Marx's own style. Even Engels's knowledge of military matters, acquired during his service in the artillery, was an asset, well used later by Marx. He admitted, as well, Engels's more rapid grasp of a subject. The partnership between the two was based on mutual admiration, a recognition by each of the other's "complementary" qualities, and on Engels's unquestionable talent as a "public relations" man for Marx.

Marx was too brilliant not to understand that he could not promote himself and needed somebody to do it. Engels's sarcastic and biting style, together with his courage, was ideal for that purpose. In a parody of Goethe's *Faust,* Engels described Marx as the leading personage. It was Engels himself who really laid the groundwork for the recognition of Marx as creator and chief of a great revolutionary movement.

Engels's penchant for destroying the idols worshiped in the sanctuary of the established order created new, extremely daring guidelines for the entire movement. His nerve and boldness were necessary to introduce into an organization of philsophically oriented middle-class intellectuals, quibbling in endless debate, an iron scaffold of a political party aiming to wrench power from all governments. He put order in the vacillating ideology of the Doctor's Club, which changed its name to The Free. He admitted openly that the young Hegelians were atheist, shaking off God, the source of order in Hegel's universal system. It was Engels who pointed out that the despised, starving, and ignorant masses were a prodigious source of power which dextrously chanelled might bring about cataclysmic changes in the world's order.

It was Engels who coined the phrase "communist party," nominating Moses Hess, another radical writer from a rich family, "Member No. 1." Why Engels's role in the movement was secondary, in spite of the fact that he possessed so many multifaceted talents, recognized often by Marx himself as superior to his own, can be explained only by the fact that Marx's dominating character could admit himself only as the uncontested "Number One."

Marx was extremely skillful in manipulating people and circumstances in his favor. Cut off completely from his family's revenues, he was able to convince, through some manipulation of figures, a group of wealthy industrialists, bankers, and traders to put up money for a liberal and progressive journal. The newspaper was to be run by their sons, young Hegelians, Marx's pals from the Doctor's Club. So was born the *Rheinische Zeitung* (Rhine Journal), a permanent platform for Marx and his group. After a short period of espousing a mild liberal tone, to satisfy the financial supporters of the newspaper, Marx outmaneuvered the moderates, proceeded twice to dismiss the manager, and hired a personal friend of his who did not possess the slightest qualification for the job.

In this way Marx obtained a tool with which he believed he could forge public opinion. Instead of creating more followers, the newspaper caused outrage and protests. Marx's brutal and arrogant style in attacking his adversaries was not of much help either, and soon the *Rheinische Zeitung* was in deep financial trouble. This was an excellent opportunity for Marx to throw the entire guilt of incompetence on his own protégé and move in himself as editor-in-chief.

Still, the newspaper's difficulties did not end. Already labeled officially as communist and subversive, in addition to shouldering financial problems, Marx was faced with the government's chicanery. Yet he was extremely dextrous in his skirmishes with the authorities. He was able to become very submissive in tone, while not giving up much of his principal line. When the official pressure increased, Marx did not hesitate to take a very moderate note, provoking an outcry from his pals that he had become "conservative." In this way Marx alternated nuances, cleverly changing from bold outspokenness to modest restraint, steering the paper through the stormy waters of continued controversy. Skillfully altering the strength of his attacks against the establishment, Marx would have been able to continue a long time with his paper.

But he soon realized that by raising the tone of his attacks and provoking the suppression of the newspaper he would gain much more in status and publicity. Becoming the martyr of reactionary persecution, a courageous knight, defending the poor and oppressed, would only enhance his reputation as revolutionary leader.

He was absolutely right that the continuing censorship and harassment of the *Rheinische Zeitung* made the newspaper more popular, but Marx wanted to get the entire credit personally, and have the fame associated only with his name. This was more difficult, as he never signed articles with his real name and preferred to keep his guiding role in the paper somewhat concealed.

When the closing of the paper approached, it became urgent to let the public know who was the real moving spirit of this fighting bastion against obscurantism and oppression. Marx wrote an article describing the entire staff of the *Rheinische Zeitung*, emphasizing his own leading role. The article was signed by a friend and published in another newspaper, *Mannheimer Abendzeitung*, and accomplished perfectly the task of acquainting the population with Marx's personality, describing it in the most laudatory terms.

With this move Marx gained in popularity, and his material position became more stable. He could marry Jenny and accept the position as editor of a revolutionary publication in Switzerland or France. He now openly professed communism as the only alternative for social development. But the brilliant perspectives soon turned sour. Marx went to Paris with the intention of publishing the *German-French Yearbook (Deutsch-Französische Jahrbücher)*. The first problem was money.

Marx was already well known for his violent biting style and ferocious attacks on the government and authorities. Even in the liberal atmosphere of Paris, trouble could be scented. Given these conditions it wasn't easy to find capital to finance the publication. With no means of acquiring cash through the underwriting of rich patrons, as had been done to finance the *Rheinische Zeitung*, Marx's associate Arnold Ruge had to use a part of his wife's fortune to finance the edition. Marx considered this a thoroughly normal obligation and was extremely annoyed because Ruge's name was mentioned on the first page. The strife became aggravated when Ruge's first investment quickly evaporated and the entire enterprise became a financial fiasco.

Marx felt that Ruge should continue to finance the paper, in spite of the fact that he didn't like or approve of Marx's vehement, caustic and acrid style. Ruge was not reluctant to call it "senseless hate" and "pure madness." And, of course, Marx was strenuously opposed to Ruge's name appearing on the first page of the paper in place of his own. To make things worse, Ruge had no high opinion about Marx's journalistic talent, and didn't make a secret of it.

All these circumstances caused the closure of the paper after the first issue. The fact that Marx with his despotic and unconciliatory character brought upon himself a moral and financial disaster, and killed his friendship with Ruge in the same way as formerly with Bruno Bauer, tells something about a destructive force impelling him to ruin his relations with his closest friends and collaborators.

Marx considered himself so superior to any of his entourage that a minimal trace of disagreement with his judgment could infuriate him. His exaggerated irascibility was also increased by his unstable financial situation, at a time when his wife was giving birth to their first daughter and needing continuous medical care because of her poor health.

The bitterness caused by his personal hardship was often expressed in the vengeful aspect of his political strategy. He preached the imperative necessity of "destruction and liquidation" as compulsory requisites to making a proletarian revolution successful. Marx couldn't liberate himself from a chauvinistic conviction of German superiority. Only the Germans, he believed, had the proper comprehension of the real mission of communism because of their preeminence in philosophy and dialectic.

A nascent friendship with Michael Bakunin, the Russian revolutionary theoretician of anarchism and one of the founders of the Internationale, also went sour, as the latter considered Marx vain, egoistic, and deceitful. Another typical aspect of Marx's character was the readiness with which he could despise an entire strata of population or a particular profession. Today we deplore the exodus of the rural populations, which creates overpopulated cities; but Marx, in his involuntary eulogies of the bourgeoisie, mentioned that it "has greatly increased the urban population as compared with the rural, and has thus rescued a considerable part of the population from the *idiocy* [italics author's] of rural life."[4] It seems incredible but this was Marx's opinion, that rural life was idiotic.

When Lenin in his inflamatory speeches addressed himself to "workers and peasants," he certainly had forgotten Marx's classification.

Was Marx at least honest, believing profoundly in what he preached and citing only facts in his propaganda? The reality is that sham and bluster were his initial tactics. From the beginning it was his idea to give an impression that the communist party already existed as a formidable international force representing members from numerous countries. In reality, it was a handful of German expatriates, characterized by Engels himself as "dumb blockheads ignorant of the most elementary mental grasp."[5] At the same time he informed Marx that they had been acting for many years as if an enormous multitude already belonged to the party, while in actuality they had only a handful of friends.

1. Introduction to *The Communist Manifesto* by Francis B. Randall. Washington Square Press, 15th printing, 1977 (New York).
2. Oscar J. Hammen, *The Red 48ers, Bonn and Berlin*, page 11.
3. Preface to the German edition of *The Communist Manifesto*, London, 1883.
4. Mark and Engels, *The Communist Manifesto*, Chapter I.
5. In a letter to Marx dated February 13, 1851.

CHAPTER V

# The Obsolescence of the Marxist Concept

How up-to-the-moment and true are some of Marx's fundamentals, now that we have neared the end of the twentieth century?

Let's scrutinize one of his basic premises:

"The proletarian movement is the self-conscious, *independent movement of the immense majority.* [italics author's.] The proletariat, the lowest stratum of our present society, *cannot stir, can not raise itself up* [author's italics], without the whole superincumbent strata of official society being sprung into the air."[1]

It is really unfortunate that in our day this kind of archaic lingo about class struggle is still attracting followers, and is a convincing medium of argumentation in the third-world countries because of the low wages that are obtained there and because of the impossibility of comparison between the capitalist and communist systems, owing to a limited access to objective media assessment. The Western proletarians, today called blue-collar workers, who have not only raised themselves up but boast of their automobiles, their own houses full of consumer-age utensils and gadgets, are incorporated into the middle class, or what Marx called in his demagogic jargon *bourgeosie.*

In the Western democracies, where the communist movement is legal and open, its party has never aroused a majority, and its independence from the communist superpowers is highly questionable. In the communist countries, where not the majority but a minority has often seized power in bloody coups, the status quo can be maintained only by the harshest police regimes of oppression. In these countries the former "superincumbent strata of official society" was in actuality "sprung into the air" when its members were killed or forced to seek refuge abroad. As a result, this elimination of an oppressive class gave way to a new superincumbent strata of the official party's bureaucracy, which has ruled in the same way as the former regimes, or even in a more autocratic way.

It is remarkable how Marx, after ascribing to the bourgeoisie many merits as a revolutionary class and bellwether of progress,[2] in a sudden twist of acrobatic dialectic, considered it as the cause and personification of all evil.

At the present stage of our civilization, which many may consider in decline, we nevertheless are witnessing a process of gradual integration of the manual labor strata into the middle class, or using Marx's terminology, of the proletarians into the bourgeosie. Moreover, in all countries where the middle class (bourgeosie) is the governing class the population enjoys the maximum of freedom, social justice and the protection of the old, the sick, and the working class. On the contrary, where the middle class has been abolished we have dictatorship either from the right or the left.

The modern Western middle class, not being an enclosed clan whose privileges are determined by birth, origin, or membership in a certain group such as the aristocracy, theocracy, or plutocracy, is in reality a loose formation with open boundaries accessible to everyone who has reached an average standard of living and culture. Consequently the blue-collar workers who send their children to college and often themselves take night courses and live in decent neighborhoods are already "in." They belong to the majority and actively influence how their country is governed. Their representatives in congress, senate, or parliament are not dummies, rubber-stamping automatically the directives either from the oligarchy or the politburo.

How ironic another of Marx's prophecies about the future communist paradise sounds today:

> "In place of the old bourgeois society with its classes and class antagonisms, we shall have an association in which the free development of each is the condition for the free development of all."[3]

Today, nearly seven decades after the establishment of the first communist state, the reality of the "free development of all" is that communist writers can not write what they think, communist painters can not paint as they feel, and communist farmers strongly attached to their piece of land, which they love, are forced to work on a state farm where their productivity is much lower. The caciques of the regime are infallible, and whoever dares to insinuate that something is not quite as it should be can expect prison, labor camp, or an asylum for the mentally insane.

Let's have a look at Marx's somewhat simplistic definition of capitalist production:

> "Capitalist production begins when each individual capital employs simultaneously a comparatively large number of labourers. A greater number of labourers working together at the same time in one place, in order to produce the same sort of commodity, constitutes both historically and logically the starting point of capitalist production."[4]

According to this definition, which Soviet group of factories (called *kombinat*), which collective (*kolchos*), or state farm (*sovchos*) are not "capitalist production"? And what of the forced labor penal camps? Marx's criteria are so out-of-date that no contemporary labor organization, be it in a free or state-directed economy, can escape his terminology of "capitalist production." No wonder that even some extreme leftists are calling the Soviet system "state capitalism."

Marx filled pages and pages with terrifying description, explaining how around 1850 labor was abused.[5] The terrible working conditions of Staffordshire potters, lace makers of Nottingham, phosphorous-match workers, and milliners' girls were described with detail, but the venerated creator of communist heaven could hardly imagine that after a century these conditions would be sad memories of the past in the Western countries, but still possible in the labor camps of communist paradise.

Another forecast absolutely inconsistent with modern technology was Marx's approach to the continuous improvement of industrial machinery, Marx's thesis, supported by comparative statistics from the years 1850 to 1862, tried to demonstrate that more modernized equipment means more and harder work for the laborer.[6] Marx, through his associate Engels — a son of a textile industrialist — was familiar with the textile industry, and particularly with the yarn-spinning sector. As a "proof" of his assertions he cited the walking distance a worker in a spinning factory should walk while attending now archaic machines called "selfactors," which moved forward and backward while the spindles twisted the yarn. The simple and "evident" proof consisted of the fact that improved machines moved quicker and the laborer, who followed the forward-backward movement, was obliged to cover more miles in his daily working hours. But Marx's genius could not foresee that a few years later the immovable spinning machine was to be invented. The spinning process, in which the laborers moved behind the moving machines (called *mules*), was abolished.

Marx quoted a report of a factory inspector in 1866 describing the working conditions at the beginning of the industrial era, which can hardly be applied to the atmosphere in all plants at the end of the twentieth century:

"Every organ of sense is injured in an equal degree by artificial elevation of the temperature by the dust-laden atmosphere, by the deafening noise, not to mention danger to life and limb among the thickly crowded machinery, which with the regularity of the seasons, issues its list of the killed and wounded in the industrial battle."[7]

If this picture is far away from a modern factory in America or Western Europe, it can still be found in the communist states, where the machinery is more obsolete than in the advanced Western countries. However, no communist regime has given a thought to changing the industrial pattern established in the capitalist world, i.e. in efforts to increase the production with fewer machines and less labor. On the contrary, the pressure on the workers through the means of propaganda, rivalry, moral, and pecuniary incentives, in order to squeeze from their working hours the maximum result, is much more intensive under the communist regimes than under the capitalist systems. Marx's description can even more correctly be applied to the state capitalism of the communist regimes than to the private capitalism of the West:

"The capitalist naturally seeks to counterbalance the decrease of the rate of profit by an increased exploitation of labor power. More must be extracted from the individual workman, consequently more value must be yielded by him, by means of prolongation of the working-day and increased strain upon his working power."[8]

Another misrepresentation was Marx's ultraromantic approach to the social changes caused by the beginning of modern capitaliam. He depicted the Middle Ages as a real paradise,[9] which was destroyed by the bourgeoisie, creator of capitalism, originating all misery and ruthless exploitation of the working class. Even the morality and sentimentalism that

Marx perceived in Medieval times were glorified by him. The world and mingling of different classes before the "domination of the bourgeoisie" was more than a symbiosis — a pure paradise, because the bourgeoisie "put an end to all feudal, patriarchal idyllic relations."[10] This deliberate distorting of historically known facts had as its objective to depict the progressive and liberal middle class as source of all evil, and an excellent target for hate and the unloading of accumulated rancor for suffering and unjustice.

The weakness of Marx's program — if we can call it such — is the discrepancy between his precision and concreteness in enumerating the evils, crimes, and deficiencies of the then existing system, and the vague nebulosity of what he proposed instead.

Another striking feature of Marx's theoretical base was the naiveté and oversimplicity of his reasoning. No wonder that the objective scholastic economist has never had a high esteem for Marx's works. Here is an excerpt from Marx's explanation of the value of labor force, and a long tirade explaining that a worker doesn't live eternally:

> "The proprietor of labour power is mortal. If such proprietors are to appear permanently on the market, and the unceasing demands of capital require this, then must that amount of labour power which is lost to the market in consequence of wear and tear or death be continually replaced by at least an equal amount of new power. The sum total of the necessaries required for the production of labour power thus includes those required by future (substitute) power, *i.e.* by the labourer's children. Likewise included in the sum total are the costs necessitated by learning the skill and dexterity requisite for a given branch of labour—costs which, however, are insignificant in so far as ordinary labour power is concerned.

"The value of labour power consists in the value of a definite amount of necessaries of life. It varies according as to how such necessaries vary — *i.e.* according to the length of working-time needed for their production. Part of these necessaries, *e.g.* foodstuffs, fuel, etc., is consumed daily and must be replaced daily. Other necessaries, such as clothes, furniture, etc., take longer to consume and need hence to be replaced only at longer intervals. Commodities of one kind must be bought or paid for daily, others weekly, quarterly, etc. But however the sum total of these costs be distributed over the course, say, of a year, it must be covered by the average income, taking one day with another. The real daily value of labour power will thus be ascertained by reckoning the value of all the necessaries of life required by the labourer during an entire year, and then dividing this sum by 365. If we assume that in the commodities required for an average day six hours social labour is contained, then does labour power represent half a day's average social work daily — or in other words, half a working day is required for the daily production of labour power. This quantity of labour necessary for the daily production of labour power constitutes the daily value of such power — or, if one likes, the value of daily reproduced power. If half a day's average social labour be incorporated also in a quantity of gold worth 75 cents, then is this sum the price corresponding to the daily value of labour power. If the proprietor of labour power offers it for 75 cents a day, then is the selling price equal to the value of such power; and we have assumed that the capitalist pays this value.

"To the peculiar nature of the commodity we call labour power is due the fact that when the contract between buyer and seller has been concluded, the value in use of the commodity in question has not really been transferred to the buyer. The value in use of labour power consists in the subsequent exercise of force. The sale of labour power and the exercise of the latter are thus separated from each other in time. But in the case of commodities, the sale of whose value in use is separated in time from their effective transfer to the buyer, payment is as a general rule made subsequently. In all countries with capitalist production the power of labour is paid only after it has exercised itself, e.g. at the end of the week. The labourer thus everywhere advances the capitalist the value in use of labour power; he lets the latter be consumed by the buyer before receiving payment of its price. Therefore does the labourer everywhere give credit to the capitalist."[11]

How out of date is this description considering the actual sophisticated bargaining tactics of the unions, choosing for stoppage the most vulnerable link in the industrial chain, to obtain not only better wages, but also stability of employment, retirement benefits, schooling, vacational facilities, etc. Entire chapters of Marx's *Das Kapital* are devoted to describing how capitalism exploits the workers by lowering wages when the offer of the labor force increases either through economic stagnation or population growth.[12] How can this argumentation be valid in industrialized countries in the time of mandatory minimum wages, unions' established guidelines, unemployment benefits, and welfare?

Let us examine Marx's descriptions of "modern" machinery and how this description applies to today's technology in the United States and Western Europe:

"All fully developed machinery consists of three essentially different parts, the motor mechanism, the transmitting mechanism, and finally the tool or working machine. The motor mechanism is that which puts the whole in motion. It either generates its own motive power, like the steam engine, the caloric engine, the electro-magnetic machine, &c., or it receives its impulse from some already existing natural force, like the water-wheel from a head of water, the wind-mill from wind. The transmitting mechanism, composed of fly-wheels, shafting, toothed wheels, pullies, straps, ropes, bands, pinions, and gearing of the most varied kind, regulates the motion, changes its form where necessary, as for instance, from linear to circular, and divides and distributes it among the working machines. These two first parts of the whole mechanism are there solely for putting the working machine in motion, by means of which motion the subject of labour is seized upon and modified as desired. The tool or working-machine is that part of the machinery with which the industrial revolution of the 18th century started. And to this day it constantly serves as such a starting point, whenever a handicraft, or a manufacture, is turned into an industry carried on by machinery.

"On a closer examination of the working-machine proper, we find in it, as a general rule, though often, no doubt, under very altered form, the apparatus and tools used by the handicraftsman or manufacturing workman. Either the entire machine is only a more or less altered mechanical edition of the old handicraft tool, as, for instance, the power-loom; or the working parts fitted in the frame of the machine are old acquaintances, as spindles, needles, saws and knives. The machine proper is therefore a mechanism that, after being set in motion, performs with its tools the same operations that were formerly done by the workman with similar tools. Whether the motive power is derived from man, or from some other machine, makes no difference in this respect. From the moment that the tool proper is taken from man, and fitted into a mechanism, a machine takes the place of a mere implement.

"The difference strikes one at once, even in those cases

where man himself continues to be the prime mover. The number of implements that he himself can use simultaneously, is limited by the number of his own natural instruments of production, by the number of his bodily organs. In Germany, they tried at first to make one spinner work two spinning wheels, that is to work simultaneously with both hands and both feet; this was too difficult. Later, a treadle spinning wheel with two spindles was invented, but adepts in spinning who could spin two threads at once, were almost as scarce as two-headed men."[13]

It is not the fact that this description can not be applied to integrated circuits, P.C. boards, solid state, synthetization, microwaves, laser beams, deuterium nuclear plants and most of the modern discoveries. The obsolesence consists in the concept that any kind of machinery is only a capitalist tool to exploit better the working class and that "in a communist society, machinery would hence be employed on a quite different scale than in a bourgeois society."[14] Actually we witness no difference in utilizing machinery in communist countries than its use in capitalist states. The dissimilarity may only consist in the fact that in the communist sphere the machinery is generally more antiquated and the authorities are feverishly trying to update it, either by direct acquisitions or by copying and stealing Western technology.

Full of contradictions and confusion is Marx's argumentation about labor hierarchy, especially its elimination by the development of machinery. His nostalgic song praising the old times of hand workmanship contradicts the aspiration of communist countries and their pride in technical advancement. Says Marx: "In modern industry one workman can easily replace another in the task of superintending the machine; and the latter can continue to operate even when the workman is sleeping or eating. Thereby the technical foundation on which is based the division of labor in manufacture, is swept away."[15] This description compares badly with the indispensable high degree of specialization necessary to operate highly sophisticated, computerized equipment. The hierarchic order of the labor force was abolished neither by technical development, nor by the capitalist system, and is maintained in communist industry.

Incomprehensible is Marx's wailing about the disappearance of higher and lower classes among the working population, as his dream was a classless society. Engels was, on the contrary, more accurate in describing the monotony and boredom of a modern assembly chain:

> "The miserable routine of endless drudgery and toil in which the same mechanical process is gone through over and over again, is like the labour of Sisyphus. The burden of labour, like the rock, keeps ever falling back on the worn out labourer."[16]

Yet this deplorable system, harming the nervous and physical system of the worker and diminishing his intellectual capacity, is copied and perfected in the Eastern bloc's factories and labor camps. Marx's attitude toward the modernization of industrial machinery is exactly the same as that of the mobs that chased Jacquard and wanted to lynch him. (Joseph-Marie Jacquard was the French inventor of the mechanical loom, able to weave large patterns, who was threatened by the hand weavers, who were afraid that his invention would put them on the street. The truth was that his invention brought more jobs and made the work much easier.) Marx stated:

> "The real facts are as follows: The labourers, when driven out of the workshop by the machinery, are thrown upon the labour market, and there add to the number of workmen at the disposal of the capitalists. In another chapter of his book it will be seen that this effect of machinery, which, as we have seen, is represented to be a

compensation to the working class, is on the contrary a most frightful scourge. For the present I will only say this: The labourers that are thrown out of work in any branch of industry, can no doubt seek for employment in some other branch. If they find it, and thus renew the bond between them and the means of subsistence, this takes place only by the intermediary of a new and additional capital that is seeking investment; not at all by the intermediary of the capital that formerly employed them and was afterwards converted into machinery."[17]

It is worth remarking that Marx's statement beginning "The real facts are as follows" was proved to be false as mechanization of the industry cheapened the product, allowing the satisfaction of wider markets and consequently increased enormously the quality of jobs and workers.

Marx and Engels's articles in the **Neue Rheinische Zeitunq** on January 13, 1849, were they to appear today, would be ridiculously false and even offensive to many nations. The articles glorify the heroic Germans and Hungarians in contrast to the barbarian Slavs, describing various peoples of the Austro-Hungarian Empire as national trash and ruins. Marx and Engels forecast that a general war would annihilate all these small ox-headed nations down to their very names. We know how erroneous were these predictions. All these little states condemned by Marx to disappear gained independence after World War I and arose as sovereign states.

Another flagrant contrast with modern reality is Marx's description of the modern worker's professional versatility. Well known is the actual, continuous, ever-increasing specialization in all domains. In a completely opposed picture, according to Marx, the working individual in a future society will no more be "a hunter, fisherman, herdsman or critic, he is this today, tomorrow that, go hunting in the morning, fish in the afternoon, be a cattle herder in evening and a critic after dinner, just as one pleased, without ever becoming a hunter, fisherman, herdsman, or critic."[18] A very attractive image, but how distant from the reality of the gray, monotonous, boring drudgery of the worker's life behind the Iron Curtain.

It is absolutely certain that Marx himself felt that some of his early ideas expressed in the *Manuscript of 1844* and destined for the *Deutch-Französische Jahrbücher* of the same year were already obsolete in 1845. In these writings Marx was much concerned with purely philosophical issues. He seriously debated with subjects such as: human essence, alienation, high humanitarian goals, disaffection of the working individual, realization of a meaningful life, and similar visionary objectives. But in *German Ideology*, which he never published (his *Early Writings* were first published in the 1930s), Marx already ridiculed thinkers with socialist overtones concerned with such trivialities as humanity and sentiment. Which is the real Marx from these two contrasting personalities? Many readers are more sympathetic to the young Marx, a humanist philosopher, than to the inflamatory demagogue of the mature years. But the obsolescence of Marx's entire thinking, regardless of whether it is the idealistic part of the early years or the pragmatic, ruthless, instigating rhetoric of his basic teaching, is mainly proved by the results obtained during the six decades of practicing his doctrine on a multinational scale. Marx knew exactly the consequences of "the dictatorship of the proletariat." The humanist justification for accepting killings, murder, terror, summary executions, restraint, suppression of the most elementary liberties, shackling of any independent thought, was the necessity to develop material conditions for an ideal society, and the creation of a new creature for the Communist Man.

Let's leave aside the determination of whether it is worth it to pay such an amount of suffering for a hypothetical and promising result, and consider only the true outcome. Marx gave a deadline ranging from twenty to a maximum of forty years for the achievement of all the ultimate goals of communism. Approaching three-quarters of a century since its practical inception, in what stage is the visionary image of an ideal communist world presently? The interminable lines in communist countries for consumer goods and certain foods have been substituted for the promised abundance for everybody. And where is the highly evolved, perfected, humanly accomplished individual, the fruit of an ideal society? The brainwashed, colorless masses, afraid not only to express an individual thought, but even to think differently from the officially prescribed line, have little resemblance to the profoundly humanist, intellectually sophisticated and articulate individual who was to be the "Communist Man" according to Marx's early vision.

Two contrasting forces influenced Marx's way of thinking and his tactical strategy in shaping the bases of a communist organizational structure. Heinrich Marx and Baron von Westphalen, father and father-in-law respectively, were deeply humanistic, impregnated with a 19th century ideology of mild nationalism, profusely tinted with liberalism, internationalism, tolerance, humanity, equality, and all the beautiful slogans that have always been mankind's aspiration. On the other hand, the boundless ambition of Marx to become a political power, in spite of a hostile, or at best indifferent environment, obliged him to use pragmatic, ruthless, and not always upright tactics. From these two conflicting influences derives the duality of two different personalities: the young idealistically inspired Marx and the mature demagogue, consciously making use of the lowest human instincts of hate, envy, and vengenance to popularize his doctrines. He never clarified completely with which kind of a new order he would substitute for the existing one. The entire attack was spearheaded against the malice, wickedness, and injustice of a capitalist society. Today, the obsolescence of this kind of scheming is so much more obvious in the light of overwhelming evidence that the ultimate goal of a leading communist state is to subjugate as many countries as possible and create a colonial empire in the most abhorrent outworn mold.

1. Karl Marx and Friedrich Engels, *The Communist Manifesto*, Chapter I.
2. *Ibid*.
3. *Communist Manifesto*, end of Chapter II.
4. Karl Marx, *Das Kapital*, Volume I, Chapter 13.
5. *Das Kapital*, Volume II, Chapter 15.
6. *Ibid*.
7. *Ibid*.
8. *Das Kapital*, Volume III, Part 1.
9. *Communist Manifesto*, Chapter 1.
10. *Ibid*.
11. *Das Kapital*, Volume I, Chapter 6.
12. *Das Kapital*, Volume II, Chapter 25.
13. *Das Kapital*, Volume II, Chapter 15.
14. *Ibid*.
15. *Ibid*.
16. Friedrich Engels, "*Lage der arbeitenden Klassen in England*" (The Conditions of the Working Classes in England).
17. *Das Kapital*, Volume I, Chapter 10.
18. Karl Marx and Friedrich Engels, *The German Ideology*.

## CHAPTER VI

# The Actual Yearning for a Truly Revolutionary Breakthrough

What mankind is actually expecting is not a listing of all present inadequacies, but an indication of an exact and realistic plan for improving its destiny. The shortcomings are well known to everybody. The deficiencies are often exaggerated. Others tend to diminish them, but nobody considers that the various governing determinants that condition our way of life are functioning perfectly. The discontent is palpably permanent, even if the force of its strain may fluctuate, indicating highs and lows. The vigorous rebellion of Western youth in the Sixties reached a force and intensity nearing a violent explosion. Their inspiration and enthusiasm for a radical change has been brutally curtailed, and their rude awakening to reality ended all illusions about bettering the existing order. Since then apathy, cynicism, and an apparent conformism have prevailed.

The older generation long ago lost any hopes that the system could be changed. No matter for whom they voted, the bureaucratic machinery has continued its implacable march, crushing between its gears any really innovative initiative. Citizenry in Western countries lost much of their interest in participating in the democratic "game," knowing in advance that not much change can be expected, since their choice is limited to candidates neither of whom is capable of fulfilling voters' expectations.

Regarding the world's political scene, it is constantly

marked by the rivalry of the superpowers. The United States, after the Viet Nam disaster, remains reluctant to engage in a new military adventure, and the entire West is on the defensive, desperately clinging to the concept of "détente," the essence of which was a pacific coexistence, without interference in the other side's affairs, and with the abandonment of attempts to expand domination. The West has more or less complied with the concept, hoping that the Soviets' fulminating offensive in different parts of the globe will somehow be decreased.

Surprisingly the Soviet Union's colonialistic process has continued to be carried on under the umbrella of liberating slogans, being at the same time ruthless in annihilating any kind of opposition, either by individuals or nations. (Allusion is made to treatment of dissidents, and armed interventions in Hungary, Czechoslovakia, Angola, and Afghanistan.) Conquest by arms and force, which is supposed to be out of fashion, has cynically continued, camouflaged by the marketing of highly ideological maxims. Again, the Marxist tenet promising redistribution of wealth is more appealing to the third world, allowing continuous expansion from the time of the Potemkin uprising in 1917 until today. From a handful of marines in Petersburg, the conquest has engulfed countries and is approaching entire continents.

The commitment by all members of the United Nations, not to use force but to settle their differences at the negotiating table, has made armed encounters more rare but has not eliminated them completely. The only difference between the older way of settling by arms any contention is the propagandistic weaponry that accompanies all clashes, while each of the litigants brandishes all the arguments that only it represents the "just and righteous cause." In spite of the U.N.'s superficial restrictions against a "robber baron's" policy, the Soviet Union's neocolonial empire is not ceasing to expand and to encompass new countries in its sphere of influence. The

West is observing this course of affairs, including the invasion of Afghanistan, somewhat passively and impotently, and any stronger reaction will be defined by Pravda as "warmongering." The talks and agreement between the two superpowers about arms limitation, which initially were aimed at gradually eliminating nuclear weaponry, and eventually arriving at a disarmament, have degenerated into a cunning haggling concerning which party will outsmart the other and be better equipped for a fatal nuclear blow. Finally the outwitted party (as usual the U.S.A.) realizes the disadvantage and wants to catch up with the artful machinator, while what was intended to be a road to disarmament deteriorated into a new and more costly arms race.

The common citizens are looking on and wondering what kind of leaders they have entrusted the world's destiny to. Disenchanted, embittered, but powerless, the citizenry is only able to ponder the fabulous expenditures that could be employed for the betterment of humankind, but are wasted in an inconclusive race of arms so terrifying that they most probably will never be used. No wonder that the more enlightened part of the masses is fed up with bombastic and empty slogans, expecting instead tangible ameliorations and real advancement in a peaceful collaboration of all humans toward the common goal of progress and prosperity.

Unfortunately, in the prevailing climate of cheating and maneuvering, such aspirations can only be regarded as overcredulous illusions. The general disbelief in moral and idealistic values engenders bitterness and cynicism. But this is only the surface of the actual current. Under the superficial crust of dispassionate indifference, a forceful stream of deep hope for a real and complete breakthrough is still alive.

The general desire is for deliverance from anxiety and fear, insecurity, distress and pessimism about a future that can be only worse than the present. Feelings are mixed and confused. The apparent conformism can only be explained as a reluctance to be considered "unrealistic," by dreaming about such impossible things as changing the status quo.

Nevertheless, the concealed flame of faith in the betterment of human destiny is still latent and ready to burst out like the lava of a volcano capable of carrying away and swaying not only youth, but everyone conscious of the unsoundness of our present global policy. For this purpose, a turn-around completely changing our values and goals is imperative. The surprising success of all kinds of gurus and even crooks and phonies preaching any sort of new religious variation indicates how eager are the masses to receive some new spiritual explanation about the true meaning of life.

The routine of amassing more and more possessions, gadgets and symbols of status does not refill the emptiness of our existence. The pressure of competition leaves the winners with a feeling of the falseness of their success — and the losers with neurotic scars. Antagonism between the "haves" and "have nots" can never diminish, be they among nations or ghetto dwellers, while the economic apparatus functions in such a way that the rich become richer and the poor poorer. Even when the desperate masses topple the upper crust, historical experience of past revolutions gives evidence that the eternal hope for betterment can hardly be realized for the entire population. As always, the privileged conditions remain achievable only for the ruling few. The topsy-turvy social upheavals, often violent and sanguinary, bearing entire countries in a mass carnage, have not accomplished their promise of alleviating the mass's fate.

The struggle for material improvement is more prominent in the developing countries. But even where the highest standards of living exist, the present generation is striving for more meaning and fulfillment in life. And they want the change for amelioration to be continuous, durable and real, not superficial and false.

In the presence of an old parliamentary system, and a deeply implanted, true democratic way of life, an armed uprising is improbable. The means of persuasion for a striking alteration shouldn't be guns, but rather reason and undisguised conviction. After more than sixty years of Communist rule in the U.S.S.R., it is difficult to hold the belief in Lenin's assurance that the dictatorship of the proletariat is the only way to democracy.[1]

How far is Soviet reality from Engels's description of the communist state in which "the need of violence against people in general, for the *subordination* of one man to another, and of one section of the population to another, will vanish altogether."[2] This promise and thousands of others equally unfulfilled, caused the prevailing mistrust of all kinds of demagogic slogans made by politicians of any color and breed. What the populace is striving for is the "true thing"—a ray of hope in the darkness of desolation, a bit of light at the end of the tunnel, a reasonable premise that tomorrow will not be worse than today, and a release from the feeling that we are walking on a descending slope. Everywhere in the Western world the magnitude of the problems is surpassing the leaders, unable to cope with inflation, unemployment, budgetary deficit, labor demands, strikes, and so many other concerns.

It is useless to throw the blame for the unbalanced economy on OPEC or the continuously increasing Soviet strength, aggressiveness and widening expansion. The young generation, which feels that its future is not secure, craves a change. The old idealistic trend of the youth forever identified as the restless hankerers for making the world more just has been identified with the practical worry about anyone's own future, so insecure in a shaky world.

This preoccupation is not the only difference between today's revolutionary tendencies and the violent eruptions of the Sixties. The failure and defeat of this glorious period—when hope was alive, confidence in the immense youthful forces capable of overcoming insurmountable obstacles, achieving unreachable goals—is still to be explained. Why has the most noble rebellion against the absurdity of a system in which the energies of everybody are used to destroy the efforts of everybody else been drowned in seas of tear gas and clubbed down with nightsticks?

Like an orchestra given the downbeat by an invisible maestro, the revolt started simultaneously in many Western countries. It could be easily explained that Moscow-trained agitators, remote-controlled from the Kremlin, wanted to blow up the capitalist system. But all the C.I.A.'s, F.B.I.'s, and Second Bureaus in the countries involved were unable to discover traces of the synchronized, coordinated work of professional instigators. The revolt was a spontaneous outbreak of a genuine rebellion against a system that, being liberal and democratic in principle, was nevertheless spiritually suffocating, exalting an all-pervading mammon worship, and despoiling the youth — by their natural disposition inclined to idealize — of any visionary inspiration of a more just and reasonable world. The system defended absurdity that must prevail at any price.

Today, brought to light by the historical debacle of the Vietnamese adventure, it is clear that the infantile brats, so resolutely opposing this war, were not at all so entirely wrong. Taming them in the name of "law and order" brought about a lot of unlawfulness and disorder. The bullets at Kent State killed not only a few students but the enthusiasm and spirit of an entire generation, which with the purest fervor wanted to give humankind the best of itself for the common betterment.

But why did they fail so sadly? Why was it so easy for a few dull and narrow-minded leaders to throttle the entire movement, which seemed to start with a force of an avalanche? The only answer is that it did not have any kind of program, any blueprint of what it proposed in place of the existing order. Not only the sheiks of the establishment, which had as its main interest sticking to the status quo, but even the citizen of the street, longing for a change, was scared to death about what would happen if the existing order were to be torn down and there were nothing positive to substitute.

Many admitted that the social structure in which we are living is obsolete and needs drastic changes. But once demolished, without any idea of what we will build in its place, are we not facing chaos, disorder, confusion, and a possible mob's rule of terror? These were the reasons why even those sectors of the establishment that might be receptive to changes remained lukewarm, and even hostile, to the movement. For them the protest was too emotional and too poorly organized.

History teaches us that all ideological movements have had practical guidelines. No important changes in any established system can be proposed without a declaration of principles and a plan of action. Similarly, as all religions have their holy books, social movements have outlined their principles to attract adherents. We expect new guidelines to be creative, nondogmatic, and predominantly humanistic. Not to be afraid to criticize alike the East or the West for weak points, shortcomings and injustices. The inspiration for the new blueprint should not derive from the holy trinity of Marx, Engels, and Lenin; but from the long chain of illuminated thinkers not excluding some true socialists such as Bebel, Liebnecht, and Rosa Luxemburg—today not only unknown but blacklisted in the Soviet Union and its satellites. The way of our thinking should be rational and analytic, not based on belief and doctrine.

The actual yearning is not to be manipulated by catch words of cloudy meaning, but to be directed by practical guidelines, adapted to actual situations. The third world, as well as dwellers of ghettos and shantytowns inside rich countries, is wondering when at least a part of the resources destined for armaments will be allocated to alleviate its plight, and is expecting tangible results instead of indoctrinating phraseology.

Therefore, unlike the Marxist dialectic materialism and *The Communist Manifesto*, which are the undisputable scriptures of the leftist ideological creed, our *Constructive Manifesto* intends to be a sketch of principles open to discussions, corrections, and improvement. The objective is, if a new rebellion erupts, not to be caught without any precise goals, and consequently in a sterile quixotic struggle. The future movement should not be limited only to the "greening of America," but to all places in both hemispheres aspiring to a progressive, just, and better world.

1. Vladimir Ilyich Lenin (Ulyanov), Section (B) of his unfinished work *The Dictatorship of the Proletariat*.
2. Friedrich Engels, "On International Topics," from The People's State, January 3, 1894.

CHAPTER VII

## *The Constructive Manifesto*

Until now, during the entire panorama of history, every revolution has begun by destroying the existing order, killing, imprisoning, torturing, or banishing the outstanding representatives of the former regime. However wrong and guilty the deposed rulers were, their cruel punishment has not prevented new wickedness and crimes. The theory that "the end justifies the means" has during history been used continuously by authorities in power to dominate those who have been deprived of power without any consideration for consent and elementary rules of justice. The maxim that "the law is in the barrel of the gun" has been equally advocated by revolutionaries and reactionaries, anarchists and fascists, freedom fighters and oppressors. All, without exception, considered themselves the only guardians of the sacred truth, empowered to administer justice and enforce their verdicts. As a result, lawlessness has followed illegality, terror oppression, ruin mischief. Abolish one privileged and parasitical stratum and another took its place, leaving the ideal of a classless society in the domain of dreams. Newcomers who have occupied ruling positions have displayed only more ignorance, rather than less wickedness. The panorama changed color, but not substance. Mistakes followed abortive experiments. The consequences of all errors were always paid by the masses, while the struggle for power at the top resulted in a kaleidoscopic change of leaders. Yesterday's heroes became villains, traitors; venerated idols, common criminals, confusing the citizen on the street, putting in doubt his own ability to judge and discern.

Taught by the historical experience of past revolutions, WE SHOULD IMPROVE WITHOUT DESTROYING.

The most common attitude of youth calling itself militant or activist is a highly critical and hostile stand toward everything that represents the established order. As, in their opinion, the entire system is wicked and wrong, anybody being a part of it, collaborating in a certain sense in its functioning, is co-responsible in the system's malefactions. Without even trying to present an alternative, the unique posture of the rebels is that of antagonism and condemnation.

Another characteristic feature predominating in the radical circles is plaintiveness about their misfortune to have had the bad luck of being stranded in such a desolate historical period where all the evil sides of human character are ascendant over the noble ones. Also common is the argument that the fault finder could do a lot about improving this catastrophic situation, but has not the "power" to do it — consequently he does nothing.

The truth concerning such an outlook is that no edifying and useful ideas can germinate from a negative stand. There have been many historical periods more perverted and wicked than ours, and only due to a group of courageous innovators, fully conscious of their objectives, did the situation change. As the exercise of power is concerned, power has never been offered as a gift. Especially in our system power is the result of hard competition between the most ambitious and gifted individuals. Even if it might be considered that the present electoral system does not give to the best individual in the nation the possibility of being elected, a better way must be outlined. Instead of continued criticism, let us CONCENTRATE ON A POSITIVE AND EDIFYING ATTITUDE INSTEAD OF A PLAINTIVE AND NEGATIVE ONE.

Two predominant contrasting social systems have emerged from the enormous variety that has been created during our entire historical evolution. Capitalism and communism have divided the globe into two opposing and hostile camps. While capitalism has accepted the principle of peaceful coexistence with the communist countries, communism, in spite of heralding détente, is continuously on the offensive, enlarging its sphere of influence in new regions. Both systems are so busy pointing out the weak side and shortcomings of their opponents that they obstinately refuse to see any advantage that the opposing system may have, even if the advantages are obvious and proven. Consequently let us ADMIT THAT ALL SOCIAL SYSTEMS HAVE SOME MERITORIOUS FEATURES THAT SHOULD BE EXPLORED AND APPLIED.

Since prehistoric times, when the human race developed tribal structures, there has emerged the necessity of leadership and discipline. To regulate society's function, rules have been established and their enforcement institutionalized. A panoramic review of all kind of authorities unfolded throughout history reveals a most contrasting variety. The range extends from the most benign and wise to the extremely tyrannic and cruel. Man's cultural level might someday reach the heights when rules, laws, regulations, and their enforcement will be unnecessary, but this stage is still far away. In the meantime, a society must be regulated by principles and the adherence to them safeguarded. Nevertheless, the established canons must be in the interests of everyone, and not favor a particular group or caste. Invoking the law should not be at the expense of human dignity, fairness, rationality, and the intrinsic sense of justice. The necessity of directing and regulating human affairs in an organized society can not justify the elimination of free speech, criticism, expressions of complaint and discontent; consequently any government should DIRECT AND REGULATE WITHOUT ENSLAVING.

Once humans accepted the principle that they should be governed, an automatic division between the rulers and ruled was created. From the dawn of history a clan or group always emerged giving orders to the predominant majority who were to obey.

The most flagrant and hypocritical untruth is the affirmation that all humans are born equal. Nobody, not even twins, is born equal. The differences are so enormous that there are no two similar individuals in the entire universe. Nature has not endowed people evenhandedly. Some are much more gifted, intelligent, clever, aggressive, and ambitious than others. Consequently, no matter which social system or circumstances we observe, we always find individuals predestined to occupy the better and more privileged positions. There will always be a superior social stratum enjoying prerogatives inaccessible to the common people. Those in power invent a complicated process to safeguard, maintain, and enlarge their privileges.

Laws, customs, rituals, precepts, and beliefs are created to form an entire system of protective walls around the prerogatives and favors enjoyed by the ruling class. The rules aiming to preserve privileges have been continuously reinforced, to such a degree that the upper class has achieved a complete mastery of the less fortunate segment of the population.

In view of the fact that human nature tends to retain, enlarge, and perpetuate preeminence and advantage, beware that NO CLASS OR GROUP HAS THE RIGHT TO INCREASE ITS DOMINATION, BY INFLUENCING THE LAWS IN ITS OWN FAVOR.

The pride of democracy is the system of free elections and the rule of majority. Most often the difference in votes between the winner and the loser is so slim that the logic of why 49.5 percent of the people should live according to the precepts of 50.5 percent is highly questionable. There is also the entire question of comparing the quality of each single vote. The democratic principle of "one man, one vote" can not discriminate one voter in favor of another, but have we all the same common sense and wisdom? We do not have in mind differences of education and intelligence, pointing toward a new superior clan of an intellectual elite, but simply differences of serenity, common sense, and sagacity among voters: a theme more broadly dealt with in the author's *Life and Voyages of the Century*. In the present electoral procedure, more than by these substantial values, the multitude can be influenced by ballyhooers, astutely using empty phrases in shrewd harangues.

Considering that we have not the minimum assurance that everything proposed and established by the majority is really in the best interest of everyone, why should the minority be obliged to live according to the precepts of the majority? The real form of freedom would be that even the smallest group could experiment with new forms of social issues. Revolutions have always been conceived as bloody and violent upheavals, where, in order to build a new social form, the old one must be razed to the ground. The experiments of the new builders were costly in time, victims, and errors. To avoid these mistakes let us ALLOW WITHIN AN ESTABLISHED ORDER A PEACEFUL WAY OF EXPERIMENTING WITH DIFFERENT APPROACHES TO IMPROVE OUR WAY OF LIFE, WITHOUT FEAR THAT ANY NEW CIVIC MOLD, HOWEVER INNOVATIVE IT MIGHT BE, WILL DESTROY ANY EXISTING VALUES OR PROVEN WAYS AND MODES.

In our opinion, the enthusiasm of the revolutionary spirit of the Sixties has been lost due to a lack of any guidelines. While we insisted on the absolute necessity of having a blueprint of principles before undertaking any action aiming at changing an actual status quo, we haven't disregarded the fact that it isn't the lack of guidelines that is plaguing mankind. During the entire historical kaleidoscope we have witnessed a real succession of enlightened spirits who unfolded to humans visions of a better life, peace, and beatitude. Strange as it may seem, the more attractive and promising was the scheme put forward, the more derided it was. In a masochistic reflex, any vision of a brighter future for mankind has been stigmatized as unrealistic and impractical. But always in the name of reason the most absurd and irrational state of affairs has been created. It will be more advisable to REHABILITATE UTOPIAN VISIONS OF SOCIETAL ARRANGEMENT AS OUR MOST NOBLE ASPIRATION OF A REASONABLE, JUST, AND LIVABLE WORLD.

On the other hand, we observe that an ideology considered effective and workable, one which was most widely chosen as the mode of revolutionary change — Marxism-Leninism — is based on nineteenth century industrial conditions so obsolete today as customs from the Stone Age. Structured on outworn, but highly inflamatory, phraseology, explained in a moth-eaten lingo, it derives its convincing force by playing on the most brutish chords of the human psyche: hate, envy, rancor, vengeance, and the destructive instinct.

A cunning mental procedure is set in motion, first by pointing out those guilty for all ills and evil. Who, if not the "haves," are the eternal cause of the suffering of the "have nots"? Even in a society without privileges of noble birth, the greater ease in achieving prominence of those born rich in comparison with those born poor is chosen as evidence of plutocratic rule. It is purposely omitted from mention that most of the great modern fortunes were created by men coming from the rank and file. Anyone with identical talents, luck, tenacity, and probably unscrupulousness, had the same chances of success. Besides, after the eventual elimination of this kind of privileged class, the void would be filled by another elite of a different kind, but with the same lust for power and prerogatives. Let us then ELIMINATE MEANINGLESS, OBSOLETE PHRASEOLOGY USED FOR DEMAGOGIC GOALS TO INCITE HATE AND CONFRONTATION INSTEAD OF A CONSTRUCTIVE COLLABORATION.

It took millennia before individuals ceased to carry personal arms for their own defense. The state had much trouble convincing citizens that they are sufficiently protected by its law enforcement organizations and don't need to walk around always bristling with weapons. But in the international community of countries, the "Wild West" order still reigns. Even the smallest and poorest states consider it mandatory to spend a huge part of their national income for armament and "defense." Isn't it time to conceive an international organization of "law and order" similar to what each country has already organized internally? Even the developing countries don't allow their citizens to flaunt guns, but superpowers and operetta states alike parade their new hardware during national holidays. Although the infrastructure of an international court exists in The Hague, it has no power to enforce its verdicts, and nations considering themselves extremely civilized mock its rulings, as did France when it was sentenced to cease open-air atomic explosions in the Pacific, and Iran when advised to release the American hostages.

Of course, appeals to empower the International Court with means to make nations respect its judgment in the form of an impartial multinational force will be immediately stigmatized as "utopian" and "unrealistic." Realistic and practical is to accelerate the armament race and burden the citizenry of the East and West equally, instead of using the trillions to alleviate their afflictions. Of course, the soundest logic of the world leaders dictates the accumulation of nuclear arms, surpassing several times the capacity of destroying everything that took thousands of years to build. No wonder today's youth, compelled to face this kind of prospective, is afflicted by malcontent and gloominess. Let's hope that a resounding call will arise TO SHIFT NATIONS FROM THE "WILD WEST" POSTURE OF FLAUNTING THEIR GUNS TO A UNIVERSAL, DULY ENFORCED INTERNATIONAL CODE OF EQUITY AND INTEGRITY.

Comparing social establishments to living beings, we must sadly concede that their actual condition is not in fine fettle. The ailments differ from one country to another, and afflictions pitilessly plaguing one government have been fully solved by another. The most common economic malaise and social unrest are nonexistent in certain spots of the globe. This special talent of particular nations to find remedies for distempers considered by others incurable should not be kept for their exclusive use and benefit. The community of nations can make good use of these particular talents in behalf of other countries badly needing solutions others could offer. As in the case of individuals excelling in a particular domain, who are called to serve the community, offering their specific endowments for the benefit of the society, so can a nation be called to a specific duty for the congregation of nations. It is time to get out from the fossilized shell of narrow-minded nationalism, and for your own benefit, lend support to others. LET US MAKE GOOD USE FOR THE ADVANTAGE OF OTHER NATIONS OF THE QUALITIES IN WHICH A SPECIFIC NATION EXCELS.

The United Nations and its organizations were created to bring countries together to settle their differences at an international forum. What is the final result? Highly politicized groups have been formed around the superpowers and among nations that believe they have common interests in achieving similar goals, or in opposing other factions. It is not an assembly unified in a common objective of eliminating animosities, eager to solve differences at a conference table instead of on a battlefield. The place can be compared to a scorpion's nest, with all around bristling their stings, ready to prick anyone supposedly having different interests. It is time to DEPOLITICIZE MULTINATIONAL ORGANIZATIONS, RESTORING TO THEM THE INITIAL OBJECTIVE OF BRINGING PEOPLE CLOSER TOGETHER.

The world realized lately and became deeply concerned with the fact that its natural resources are limited and nearing exhaustion. Statistics concerning how many years a determined raw material will suffice have been gathered. It caused much surprise and alarm when it was realized how limited is the time of the duration of our resources. Voices about substituting, saving, and reducing the consumption have been abundant. But wasting has not ceased and reasonable priorities have not been established.

Millions of petro-guzzling cars are still on the roads, while ghettos, slums, shantytowns still exist and plans for the development of many emerging nations have been shelved, their budgets incapable of balancing the cost of oil imports. Misery, despair, subhuman living conditions exist as close neighbors with extremes of abundance, senseless waste, frills, and overplentifulness. The same phenomenal contrast can be observed between districts in the same city, as well as between countries on the same continent.

The outcry of the underprivileged for sharing at least partially in the wealth, be it by minority groups within a country or the third world in the community of nations, becomes continuously more intense. The contrast between the countries with abundance and the countries suffering starvation from malnutrition, high death rate caused by lack of adequate medical and hygienic facilities, children working in mines, and economic recession in rich countries due to overproduction of goods, difficult to place in a saturated market, is significant.

This picture has become a common pattern in industrialized societies, as well as in the entire world structure, among nations. Thus as we strive to eliminate crime, poverty, ignorance, and injustice inside a land, a world-wide constructive plan to deal with the problem on a global scale should be conceived. If we visualize a future humanity where misery is eliminated once and forever, the shaping of a new mentality is compelling. Foreign aid, in the form of charitable donations, ending up in the pocket of a corrupted bureaucracy is not the answer. The future belongs to a society of nations, instead of a society of classes. As every country tries to raise the level of its "lumpenproletarians" (the name given by Marx to the social scum, the "dangerous class," the lowest layers of society) and integrate them into a regularly employed working class, the community of nations is committed to design a comprehensive plan, and ESTABLISH PRIORITIES IN USING RESOURCES TO ALLEVIATE THE STRUGGLE, BE IT FOR UNDERPRIVILEGED MINORITIES WITHIN A COUNTRY OR FOR DEVELOPING COUNTRIES.

Concerning the abortion problem, the two opposing factions have chosen different slogan-banners under which they engage in a ferocious combat. The partisans of free abortions are calling for the "right to choose" and the adversaries are fighting for the "right to life." Neither faction represents reality.

The maternal instinct is strong enough to cause the future mother to agree to endure all sufferings and hardships connected with her biological mission. When in spite of and contrary to the natural drive to become a mother, the decision to abort is made after an intense internal struggle, it is not the result of a "free choice." The mother-to-be is most often an unmarried teenager, without resources to raise a child, surrounded by a hostile, prejudicial environment, unprepared to fully accept single parenthood. She is without freedom of choice, but pushed and obliged to abort.

The opposition to abortion, which invokes the hypocritical slogan "the right to life," and claims the authority to guard with policemen women's wombs, also carries a false banner in its crusade. Are they really fighting for the future life of children and adults who may grow from an inseminated ovule?

It's easy to proclaim partisanship for life, but what kind of life? What is the contribution of these "right-to-lifers" toward making the future lives of these children bearable? If this affection for life were unfaked, instead of there being all kinds of legal hindrances for the poor in obtaining an abortion, help for the mother-to-be would be advocated. In substance the entire problem exclusively concerns the poor, as the rich never have had a problem in obtaining abortions at will, always able either to find a physician willing to perform the procedure or to travel to a foreign country where no abortion restriction exists.

Instead of pushing the desperate pregnant girl into the hands of a shadowy abortionist, let's give her all the protection she so badly needs. Instead of legal battles, we propose:

Schools for pregnant teenagers in which they can continue their studies without attracting attention to their condition;

Full esteem and respect for motherhood, independent of marital status;

Financial assurance that the child will be raised with all necessary care in a loving and propitious atmosphere;

Temporary adoption, without the natural mother losing trace of her child and with the right to claim her child when she obtains financial independence and ability to support her offspring.

NO LEGALITIES CAN BE INVOKED TO INTRUDE IN THE WOMAN'S INALIENABLE RIGHT TO DETERMINE THE FATE OF HER OWN BODY OR PART OF IT, EVEN IF IT IS AN INSEMINATED CELL.

Often viewpoints are voiced that the precarious world situation is caused by the rivalry of the two superpowers. Their continuous clashes endanger world peace and may lead to a nuclear confrontation, tantamount to the end of our civilization. In the interest of preserving peace, the existence of a third power, balancing this antagonism might be of uppermost importance. A hope has come in sight, that the European Common Market will rapidly evolve into a federal union of European states, creating a formidable technological and economic power able to soften the dangerous wrangling between the U.S. and Russia. Illusions disappeared in no time when conflicts of nationalistic interests made it clear that a realization of a unified European political body still has a long way to go to be realized. Nonetheless, an European parliament has been formed, plans for a single currency are under study, and the hopes of finally transforming Europe into a single political entity have not been abandoned. To mute Soviet expansionism, equivalent to strengthening world peace, a strong homogenous western European bloc is imperative. EUROPEAN COMMON MARKET MEMBERS AND THEIR ALLIES SHOULD ABANDON NATIONALISTIC BICKERING AND SPEED UP THE INEVITABLE CREATION OF THE UNITED STATES OF EUROPE.

When the word détente has been used to describe the thaw of the ice-cold relationship between the West and the U.S.S.R., the entire world has clung to a newly awakened hope: that finally the eternal bickering will cease, relations will be smoother and harmonized to a mutual, obvious, and enduring advantage. None of the seasoned veteran Western diplomats suspected that the newly coined expression for amicability would be cunningly used by the Russians to obtain the most without giving anything in return. Western technology has bolstered and reinvigorated the formidable Soviet war machine; trade and credit have rejuvenated its aging industry; huge, low-interest, long-term loans to the Russian satellite states have muted the discontent of their populations concerning scarcity and the high prices of consumer goods. The West has done everything in its power to strengthen and solidify its new "friend."

Have all these actions induced gestures of good will and curbed Soviet expansionism and predominance? Formerly we had the bloody suppression of the rebellion in Hungary, the invasion of Czechoslovakia. Now we have the using of Cuba as a military base, and its army as proxy mercenaries in Angola, Ethiopia, and South Yemen — all these acts have been committed to the tune of the sweet lullaby of détente.

There have been some politicians who have cautioned the public that détente is a one-way street with all the advantages for the Soviets. Their warnings have been disregarded, as the general trend has been that easing tension with the mighty Eastern neighbor is in the interest of the West. Of course it is, but only in an honest give-and-take arrangement, without treachery, cynicism, and hypocritical self-pride by one side of itself as the "defender of liberty" and the other side as the "imperialist oppressor." Objective observation of the Kremlin's tactical strategy on the world's chessboard during the last decade makes it difficult not to reach the conclusion that Russia is the last colonial empire on the globe. There is no other government that dominates so many different nationalities and countries under its uncurbed domination. The theoretical premise that the Soviet Union is a voluntary federation of independent republics does not make much sense in light of the facts — that any single individual who dares to speak out against such a union will be gagged and sent to prison.

The servile and obliging attitude of the Warsaw Pact states, always going along with and praising any Soviet move, should also be explained by the hundreds of Soviet armored divisions stationed throughout the countries of its influence. What might be the real and uncoerced posture of these lands could only be determined if the Kremlin's troops were withdrawn.

Let's have courage and face reality. Machiavelli's principle "divide and conquer" is masterfully applied by the Soviets. The West has never been able to present a unified, cohesive front with a common objective and strategy. There has been no understanding of the basic principle that a group of nations with common interests needs a leader, as does a group of soldiers, let alone one who will eventually guide the team. The sole presumption that it should be the United States has made the entire idea unpalatable for some European participants. As a result, in response to the clearly defined, skillfully orchestrated, aggressively expansionist policy of the Kremlin, we have from the western side a chaotic, uncoordinated, quivering, fearful, and contradicting reaction. No wonder Russia is on the offensive and the West beats a shameful and disastrous retreat.

It is time to realize that there is no limiting border where the Russian ideological and territorial assault will stop, arrested by its own restraint. Their ideological crusade is only a part of the impelling force to expand everywhere. The major cause of the formidable increase in the technological potential of the Soviet Union is the annexation or incorporation into its orbit of several European countries. Many of the satellites were culturally and industrially more developed than Russia, contributing conspicuously to the furtherance of the Soviets. More conquests of, or association with, industrially developed countries will alleviate the chronic shortages of consumer goods. Military and technological aid to developing countries gives the Soviets footholds for strategic expansion. The use of Cubans as proxy fighters for Soviet interests in different parts of Africa caused less international swirl than the direct invasion of Soviet armored divisions in Czechoslovakia and Afghanistan. It is imperative TO REDEFINE THE MEANING AND MUTUAL OBLIGATIONS OF DÉTENTE, PUTTING AN END TO THE UNILATERAL ABUSE OF THE MOST SUBSTANTIAL BASICS OF THE CONCEPT.

From time immemorial the big power game of expanding their sphere of influence has been a favorite habit pattern. Assured by their predominant military strength and the lack of any significant resistance, the choice of terrain has been dictated by strategic, economic, or other political motives. The sentiments of the indigenous population and their sufferings and casualties during the process of conquest have never been taken into consideration.

Unbelievable as it may seem, this barbarian conduct is pursued to the very present moment. Viet Nam under the Americans, Cambodia under the Vietnamese, Afghanistan under the Russians are examples in which in the name of so-called "national interest" an independent country is overrun, its land, heritage, and villages destroyed, and the population slaughtered or displaced and famished. An assault on a single person is a criminal act, punishable with long-term prison. Chiefs of state, who with a sole shake of a pen are responsible for the decimation of entire nations, are, meanwhile, getting away with it, uncastigated, and often even rewarded and honored. WE HOPE THAT THE DAY MAY NOT BE FAR OFF WHEN AN INTERNATIONAL ENFORCEABLE LAW WILL BE ENACTED PROHIBITING AND PUNISHING ANY OVERRIDING OF A FOREIGN COUNTRY AND VICTIMIZATION OF ITS POPULATION.

Nationalism of any sort is one of the greatest obstacles to a harmonious and peaceful cohabitation in the community of nations. To cherish a folkloric heritage is an unrestricted sentimental privilege, but biasing it into a prejudicial chauvinism is the first step to despicable racism. National pride is easily distorted into a sense of superiority over other nations and always has served throughout history as a justification for bellicose adventures, conquests, and oppression. The final destiny of this globe is either a peaceful cooperation of all nations or an end to the human race in an apocalyptic destruction. Time and resources are continually wasted to settle petty differences, instead of being used to structure a collaboration of all nations in which each nation's contribution will benefit the whole. TO SHIFT THE GIGANTIC RESOURCES EMPLOYED IN ARMAMENTS INTO PRODUCTIVE AND BENEFICIAL GOALS, THE EFFORTS TO UNIFY NATIONS IN COMMON CONSTRUCTIVE ENDEAVORS SHOULD BE OF FIRST PRIORITY.

Evolving into a complicated and interrelated society, individuals have renounced a good deal of their freedom, subordinating themselves to rules and restrictions, enabling the functioning of an organized community. To safeguard and regulate the conformity to the established guidelines, a supervising clan was necessary. Independently, if this directing group was elected or self-appointed, its mission was to be submissive to the ultimate necessities of the society. Bureaucracy became ancient as well as modern society's necessity. The unfortunate part was its disproportionate growth and ever- increasing dominating role. It is paradoxical that an element destined to be instrumental in lightening our burdens became an entity per se, with its own interests; and before engaging in a specific social task the bureaucracy, according to the laws of self-preservation, strengthened its own position and influence. WE SHOULD NEVER ALLOW THE SPIRITLESS BUREAUCRACY TO DOMINATE THE VITAL HUMAN NEEDS, INSTEAD OF SERVING THEM.

The entire Western world is under continuous pressure from the Kremlin's expansionist policy. In spite of being overwhelmed by economic problems, most of the Western countries are obliged to carry the heavy burden of military upgrading, as hopes of a mutually gradual demilitarization have vanished. The picture looks grim and despairing. Nevertheless there is a possibility that might seem an optimistic dream but lies within reach.

In reality, the two ferociously contrasting ideologies are not so distant from each other as they believe. The modern world, without realizing, has been dragged into an archaic kind of holy war in which the adherents of Marx on one side and the followers of Adam Smith on the other have not excluded a mutual annihilation in the name of their principles. This is the essence of the problem even if it does seem ridiculous and incredible. After a closer look down the historical path of both ideologies it is evident that they are on a convergent course.

Pure capitalism, in its original form, is disappearing. Personal or family industrial empires become more rare, and the lion's share of the profits does not necessarily go to the ownership. Practically, a type of cooperativism has been created de facto between ownership, state, and workers. The communist camp has also changed considerably. The initial plan for reaching ideal communism, after a brief socialist period, has been scrapped. Without terminating the socialistic phase, state capitalism took its place.

The two blocs, which so vehemently reject each other's ideology, fail to see how close they are from the socioeconomic point of view. The solution to the world's problems does not lie in the fact of which side is better armed, or in the behavior of certain politicians, but in the eliminating of the core of antagonism. The supposedly diametrically opposed ideologies give the grounds for continuous confrontation and combativeness. Once the ideological basis of hatred is eliminated, completely new horizons of mutual cooperation will be opened to a reciprocal benefit.

SINCE THE CONTRASTS BETWEEN THE COMMUNIST AND CAPITALIST SYSTEMS ARE CONTINUOUSLY DIMINISHING, A NEW INTERMEDIATE SOCIAL SYSTEM, ACCEPTABLE TO BOTH, WILL ELIMINATE THE REASON FOR COMBATIVENESS AND FRICTION, MAKING POSSIBLE A REAL AND SINCERE COOPERATION AMONG NATIONS.